Crime Scene Investigation: CSI

The Unauthorized Guide to the CBS Hit show
CSI Miami: Season One

By: Kristina Benson

The Unauthorized Guide to the CBS Hit Show CSI Miami: Season One

ISBN: 978-1-60332-024-5

Edited By: Brooke Winger

Copyright© 2008 Equity Press. No part of this publication may be reproduced, stored in a retrieval system, or transmitted in any form or by any means (electronic, mechanical, photocopying, recording or otherwise) without either the prior written permission of the publisher or a license permitting restricted copying in the United States or abroad.

The scanning, uploading and distribution of this book via the internet or via any other means without the permission of the publisher is illegal and punishable by law. Please purchase only authorized electronic editions, and do not participate in or encourage piracy of copyrighted materials.

DISCLAIMER: This book is unofficial and unauthorized. It is not authorized, approved, licensed, or endorsed by CBS, Viacom Inc., its producers, writers, distributors, publishers, or licensors. Any use of the trademarks and character names is strictly for the purpose of analysis and news reporting. All material related to the analysis is © CBS © Viacom and © Jerry Bruckheimer © CSI

Trademarks: All trademarks are the property of their respective owners. Equity Press is not associated with any product or vender mentioned in this book.

Printed in the United States of America

Table of Contents

Table of Contents 3

Episode Guide 5

    The Golden Parachute 7

    Losing Face 19

    Wet Foot/Dry foot 29

    Just One Kiss 41

    Ashes to Ashes 53

    Broken 65

    Breathless 79

    Slaughterhouse 91

    Kill Zone 103

    A Horrible Mind 113

    Camp Fear 121

    Entrance Wounds 132

    Bunk 139

    Forced Entry 145

    Dead Woman Walking 152

    Evidence of Things Unseen 157

Simple Man 163

Dispo Day 171

Double Cap 181

Grave Young Men 189

Spring Break 195

Tinder Box 201

Freaks and Tweaks 205

Body Count 211

INDEX 219

Episode Guide

CSI Miami: Season One

The Golden Parachute

The sun hovers over Miami as a small plane, drawing a line of smoke over the horizon, crashes and explodes.

In the next shot, Horatio Caine and Eric Delko arrive at the wreckage. Delko, putting on his Captain Exposition hat says, "Flight 906, outbound Miami to D.C., dropped off the radar at oh-eight-twenty. Crashed right after takeoff...NTSB [national transit safety board] confirms two pilots, six passengers."

Caine immediately starts barking orders: "tell then I want to set up a forward command post at levee 67 -- mobile recovery, biohazard gear, the works. And then call in the night shift. We need all hands on deck." He is momentarily distracted and then his tone changes: "Right there, we've got a survivor right there!" Delko leaps in the water, arms pumping furiously until he reaches the man. "He's not breathing!" he wails, and drags him ashore to launch into CPR. Delko screams at the man and practically tries to force him back to life, but it doesn't work. He gives up and the man's status moves from Survivor to Victim.

The credits slide down the screen to open the first scene of of Caine and Calleigh. We learn that jet was registered to a Scott Eric Sommer, who made the Fortune 500 by way of dabbling in insurance scams. While they discuss which emergency and law enforcement agencies are coming from where and how long they will take to get there, Delko has the less glamorous job of wading through the swamp where the plane crashed, looking for remains. While he deals with an arm floating dismembered in the water, Megan Donnell and Tim Speedle arrive. We learn that in addition to being the site of a plane crash, they area may be contaminated with hazardous materials from the jet fuel, making it a " level two biohazard site." In addition to wearing hazmat gear, everyone must take antibiotics, refrain from taking food and water to the site, and break after twenty minutes of work to decontaminate.

Megan strolls purposefully over to Horatio to ask if he thinks it's a bomb. He welcomes her back, and tells her he isn't sure yet. Megan purses her lips disapprovingly before reminding him that he doesn't really have jurisdiction on this since it's an air crash. They deputize local agencies which means Miami PD works for them. Not the other way around. He doesn't really seem to care. They have a terse exchange and he offers Megan her old job back; she declines and he walks off.

The next scene is of a makeshift morgue, presided over by Alexx the coroner. She notes that the victim has injuries consistent with this type of crash, but points to a corpse and shows Horatio a bullet wound. A .32 or .38 entered him, then exited. He then calls for Calleigh, and asks her to see if there is a bullet in the fuselage.

Meanwhile, Megan and Speedle watch a policeman interview a fisherman who had scene the plane crash and called 911. Speedle notes the rifle in the boat and opines that they are going to poach alligators. Megan lectures him on what happens when you assume thing . Then she tosses her head and walks off in high heels that are ridiculously impractical for a swamp.

She walks over to Horatio and combs through the grass with him for evidence. He immediately holds up a piece of twisted metal and points out the fact that the part's serial number has been sanded off, indicating that an old airplane part was sold as new. Megan, forgetting her demotion, says "I'll have Speedle look into it." Horatio rebuts, "I need Speedle here for collection." Megan pauses and looks upset and finally says, "I'll look into it."

Later, Megan, Horatio, Delko, and Speedle reconvene and examine the muddy plane chair lying on its side, its seatbelt is unbuckled and undamaged. He elaborates on why this was significant: "I've counted nine unbuckled belts, so that would mean one of the passengers was unbuckled during takeoff, doesn't it?" Then he stumbles upon a red briefcase with a "CMC" monogram, and takes it to the makeshift lab that's been set up on the site.

He pries the briefcase open, but it's empty. Off in the distance, Delko finds another survivor and once again administers CPR incorrectly. After commercial break, he's put in an ambulance. As Horatio watches it go, he muses that since he has no friction burn from the seatbelt, he may be the shooter.

Megan interrupts him to tell him she found a floater, and he soon finds himself staring at the body of a woman, her clothes stained with blood, floating in the water in a bizarre pose. They take her to the morgue where Alexx, as is her habit, begins talking to the body: "How did you get so far away from your friends? Did you fall out of that plane? Is that how you ended up all alone out there? All by yourself?" Horatio has already gotten the passenger manifesto. She was the only woman on board. He identifies the body as Christina Maria Colucci.

Alexx continues the exam while Horatio watches from a window above for reasons that are totally unknown. Because there is no friction on her torso, Horatio deduces that Christina also wasn't wearing her seatbelt, and that although it was 8 o'clock in the morning when her plane crashed, her blood alcohol is point-oh-nine. The tox screen also indicated that she was on prozac. On Christina's hand there are deep, perfectly circular marks, cause unknown.

In the next shot, Horatio has the unfortunate duty of telling Mrs. Collucci that her daughter died. In a scene that is supposed to be very touching as indicated by the emotional music in the background, he learns that she recently got the red briefcase as a gift for her promotion, that she battled depression in high school, and that she was good at keeping secrets.

Over at the plane's fuselage, Calleigh explains to a bit player who doesn't have a name that she is there to gather ballistics evidence. She puts on her Exposition Hat and tells him, "We think there may have been a shooting on the plane, but so far, nada." She flirts with him, and learns that he is the Airplane Guy. (She is the Bullet Girl.) They poke around together and find that the pins that hold the door on the plane are marked by vertical scores.

Back at the lab, Horatio and Speedle discuss the purpose of the doomed flight: they were being investigated by the Securities and Exchange Commission. As they discuss this, Calleigh comes in and shares the news that the bayonet pins were shot and the plane door opened mid-flight, which would explain how Christina ended up five miles from the crash. Horatio starts beat boxing and says

"Telling all y'all it's a sabotage!". Kidding. But he does say it might be sabotage. Speedle considers this a viable theory: "Company's in trouble, lot of employees ticked off at the boss..." Calleigh finishes: "Exit door pins were tampered with, most likely by someone who knew their way around a jet aircraft." They decide to find out who worked on the plane.

The man in question is a Cuban or perhaps Puerto Rican American whose grasp of English is lacking. Still, however, he communicates that yes he did that to the bayonet pins but only cause he wanted to make them fit. They eventually let him go after they learn that the plane only got to 4000 feet, so the cabin never depressurized, which means the door couldn't come off by itself. This means it was suicide, or murder.

Someone finally decides to interview the lone survivor, Scott Summer. He learns that no one else survived and says firmly, "We'll take care of their families. We take care of our own." Megan nods thoughtfully, lets him know that she knows that he was under the investigation by the SEC, and asks for his DNA. Horatio assures Sommer he need to lawyer up, and that he and Megan are merely trying to establish what really happened from his point of view. He finally spits out "I didn't want to anything because I was trying to protect her. Christina was acting strangely that morning. She was very agitated, and she had been drinking..." We go immediately to flashback cam and see Christina wash down her Prozac with bourbon, and then heads to the door and gets sucked out. Oh and he didn't hear a gunshot.

At the CSI headquarters, they decide to see if Christina was truly acting irrationally due to a fatal drug combination. They do a drug hair test to get an idea of what she was doing and when. They learn that Christina had been on antidepressants for about a year, and had smoked some pot six months ago.

Megan decides that this all means she must have committed suicide. She follows Horatio shrieking "mass spec doesn't lie! She was the focus of an SEC investigation, she knew where all the bodies were buried, maybe she couldn't live with that...she tried to kill herself three months ago." Horatio isn't buying it. He does start musing, however, on the fact that she could have been a whistleblower, since most whistleblowers are women. Megan wonders if she was going to take the company down, and then says, in any case, "Her testimony died with her."

As they argue—Horatio deciding that Christina was murdered, Megan saying that shooting the pilot is a dumb way to murder someone. Speedle and Delko watch from the glassed-in safety of the lab. Delko says "What does she think, she can waltz in here after six months of being gone and just take over?" Speedle rolls his eyes and says "She lost her husband? What did they give her, two weeks off? She needed a little bit of time. Big deal." They are interrupted from the gossip by getting ordered to look again for the black box.

At the same time, Horatio and Megan use a blacklight and discover that Christina and Sommer's handprints are all over the inside of the door. They reenact every possible scenario, but the only one that matches the prints is the one in which Summers pushes Christina out.

Later, Speedle and Delko have retrieved the black box from a pool of alligators. They gather around to listen, and hear the chatter of the pilot and copilot. The first four minutes after takeoff were normal. Four minutes in, it changes a bit:

"This is the captain. Our flight to Washington, D.C., is two hours, twenty minutes. The temperature is 72 degrees."
[loud noise]
"What was that?"
"We've got a light on. Could be electrical."
"Exit light is definitely on. We've got a door open."

"What the hell's going on back there?"
"Losing power."
"Got a warning light -- engine two!"
"We're losing air speed!"
"We lost number two!"
"Pull out, pull out!"
"Can't get --"

Calleigh immediately says:"There's no gunshot." The loud noise was the door. The audio tech somehow brings up the noise in the background and mutes the pilot's voices. We hear:

Man: I'm not going to let you --
Woman: Get off of me!

We hear Christina screaming, and then only the engine. Christina held on for seventeen seconds before being pushed out. Horatio immediately starts barking orders: Speedle is to go to Christina's apartment, Calleigh is to head back out into the swamp to examine the airframe, and Delko is to focus on the number two engine to see what brought down the plane.

Speedle discovers that Christina left no normal premeditated suicide signs. Calleigh finds an interesting looking hole. Delko stares really really hard at the engine.

Then Calleigh finds a bolt that looks like it caused the pilot's injury, Delko finds a red fiber in the engine, and Speedle finds a slip for an express delivery.

Calleigh tells us that one red suede shoes caused the crash. As Christina fell out of the plane, her shoe was sucked into the engine. Fingerprints found on the fire extinguisher indicate Summer beat her knuckles till she let go and fell. As for why other passengers didn't help her: Speedle recounts the theory of whistleblower isolation versus the old-boys' business club: "Sommer knew nobody on the plane was going to testify; they were all on the payroll. It would be against their own interests."

They go to arrest Summers but he's already dispatched himself to the great hereafter, having hung himself from the rafters. Horatio tells Christina's mother that she mailed a report to the SEC the morning she died.

And of course, we get to hear the letter in the report: "To whom it may concern: I hope I'm not writing this letter in vain, but I feel I have a responsibility to those who depend on us, to those who expect us to deliver honest and fair accounting. I feel a responsibility to speak the truth for those innocent victims who are powerless to speak it themselves, because without the truth, we ourselves are powerless."

CSI Miami: Season One

Losing Face

Day breaks over Miami, and an anchorman primps in preparation for his morning show. Somewhere else in Miami, a woman is sleeping while an unseen speaker whispers "Julisa". The alarm goes off 6 a.m., and she opens her eyes and says "Aurelio?" Clearly she is under the impression that this Aurelio person is supposed to be in the bed with her. As Julisa pads down the hall, she hears her name in the same whisper. In Spanish, she asks "What are you doing here?" Aurelio chose not to go to bed last night apparently, and spent the evening in a chair. He has PVC pipe around his neck and a note pinned on his chest that says:

this is a
BOMB
deliver 50,000 dollars
in the next four hours
put the money in a brown paper bag
call 555-0187
do not call the police

Not very good at following directions, she calls the police and several black and whites screech to the house. Horatio steps out of a HumVee and enthusiastically greets Al, another police type, and we learn that Aurelio had a

Schedule-80 PVC collar clamped around the his neck. Al is going in the house to defuse it by hand.

Al's professionalism clearly does not put the victim at ease. Aurelio trembles and says "Would you tell my wife...tell her I love her." "I'm kind of busy at the moment," snaps Al. "You can tell her yourself in a few minutes. You two will be knocking back mojitos in no time." As Al goes to work, we are shown an exterior shot of Horatio examining an X-ray of the bomb. As he does so, the bomb detonates and blows out the windows of the house.

After the commercial break, Calleigh, Speedle, Megan, and Delko arrive. Megan walks into the house first and Horatio is examining what is left of the victim and of his good buddy Al. He says: "The victim's name is, uh, Aurelio Moreno. He's a...successful...Colombian importer. This is obviously the seat of detonation right here. The shattering effect here indicates high explosive and frag pattern indicates that the explosive was, uh, was packed up front. Everything above the neck blown away. Below remains intact." Megan asks him if he will be able to impartially work the case and he assures her that he will, and continues listing the damage: the heads were blown off but the bodies are intact. There is frag from the container itself, thermal effect from the release of the gasses, and blast pressure. The blast pressure, Delko explains, is potentially the most damaging. Blast pressure forces air outward in a shock front of up to 29,000 feet per second. Blast pressure has two phases -- positive and negative. When the air is pushed outward, it creates a vacuum in the center. So everything gets sucked back in. Horatio tells his crew that this also means that the components of the device are in the room, shattered into a thousand pieces, and that they need to start gathering them. He then begins barking orders: "So, Calleigh, let's find out who had access to the house, Eric, we've got to find that ransom note, and Speed, you, Megan and I will look for the bomb."

They get to work. We see Calleigh find a tiny piece of honeycomb-like fabric caught in the door jamb and pulls it down. She then tells Horatio, "the bomber came in through an unlocked window in the maid's room. Yesterday was her regular day off. Moreno's wife said he liked to stay up late and watch TV. My guess is, he got jumped right in the middle of Letterman." Delko found the note, which is legible despite the fact that it's splattered with blood and slightly burnt. Horatio has found Al's wedding ring, and instead of bagging it and sending it to the evidence room, tells Megan he will be giving it to Al's wife. Megan appears to disapprove but says nothing.

At the morgue, Alexx examines the body and says: "Avulsive destruction of the face and frontal calvarium.

Thermal damage to the epidermis at the edges of the defect." There are traces of chloroform in Moreno's system. The exterior of his body below the neck looks fine but Alexx pulls back his skin and we see what looks like spaghetti marinara. "White butterfly effect", she explains. Overpressure can cause massive internal damage. Lungs burst. Other organs turn to soup."

After Horatio tells Al's widow and her children that Al blew up, we cut to a scene of Megan and Horatio examining the bomb pieces. Horatio concludes the bomb maker was a pro, and reprimands his crew for failing to bring him the action switch. In the next shot, Horatio is examining the sole of a firefighter's boot, and Speedle delivers more boots, explaining that there will be more where that came from: three separate engine companies responded to the bomb call.

Calleigh, in the meantime, has analyzed the fabric from the doorjamb: French lace. Delko then enters to report what he's learned about the ransom note: "I ran thin-layer chromatography on the ink. It's a garden-variety laser printer, and you can find them at any copy shop. It made me realize I was barking up the wrong tree...[the paper] is bagasse pulp -- a treeless fiber. It's made from sugarcane pulp, it's imported primarily from Colombia..There are four high-end stationery stores in Dade County. All of them are sold out, and they're awaiting a shipment from a Colombian import company that's owned by one Aurelio Moreno. And I did some other fact checking. There's been a string of necklace bomb cases just like this one in and around Bogota. The bombers stalk their victims for weeks, get their routines down cold. They pick only high-profile targets that are wealthy enough to pay the ransom." The crew then does research and finds out that some of the paper is impounded in Customs.

The next shot is of Delko at a warehouse, telling the manager that he's looking for "Coded watermarks... a design pressed into the liquid paper stock. It can tell us when a particular lot was manufactured." He finds paper with matching watermarks, and asks who has access to the paper. Apparently, a lot of people: security guards, dockworkers, plus any number of Federal inspectors on a regular basis. Delko asks if there's a file on Moreno, and there is. They retrieve and read the file. We come to a photo of a good looking Latina and Delko identifies her as Wife Number 2: Lauriana.

At the lab, Horatio gives us a lesson on explosives: "For a bomb to do its job, it needs three components. It needs a power source, it needs an action switch, and it needs an explosive load." So they wired in a photocell like the one we found melted into the fireman's boot. Horatio conintinues,

"So, Al followed a render-safe procedure, and he drilled in, in an attempt to disrupt the power source...Once the pipe was breached, the light hit the photocell and closed the circuit...Bombers are ego-driven. They make bombs to gain control, get revenge, sow terror. Some believe they've been betrayed by society." Delko feels that Moreno's wife may have been relevant to the crime. Wife#2 is in town, so Horatio decides to pay her a visit.

Wife Number 2 is Julisa. She says: "I don't know anyone who would want to hurt him. He was hard-working. Aurelio was a good man, honest. He loved his family. "Of course he had to travel for business, but he hated it. He didn't like to be away from me." Meanwhile, Lauriana (who is wearing a French lace blouse) is telling Megan, "My husband was very devoted to family. He traveled quite a bit, but he hated to be away from us. If there was even a weekend he could get away, he would come home. He never wanted to leave me. I miss him so much." Megan asks to swab Lauriana's hand and Horatio wants to swab Julisa. We see their hands in two back-to-back shots and see that they have the same manicure and the same wedding band set. After the interview, Mrs. Moreno 1 and Mrs. Morena 2 wait for the elevator -- Lauriana in a black top and white skirt, Julisa in a white top and black skirt. They seem to be totally oblivious to the presence of the other.

When they get the lab results back they learn that Julisa's hands were clean, but Lauriana had trace elements of triacetone and triperoxide (TATP). He says already called INS to detain Lauriana. Megan sighs and after a long, soporific monologue about the dangers of mixing work and grief, says: "Did you notice Lauriana's hair and nails? Acetone and peroxide. Base elements of TATP. Also of nail polish and hair dye. Those two women didn't bat an eye on the elevator. I'm a woman and I'm telling you, they don't know each other. They probably have no idea the other exists." Horatio's cell phone rings. "We've got another bomb," he announces.

The victim this time is one Maura Burgos who's an antiques dealer. Meanwhile, Horatio's talking to Cabera— the new bomb tech person now that Al blew up-- over walkie-talkies, asking how Burgos managed to contact the police. Cabera tells him that Burgos used her garage door opener to open and shut the door over and over again until a neighbor came over to see what was going on. Horatio, who has looked at an X-ray and has seen that this bomb is like the other, tells Cabera that the "safe arm" of the bomb is on the right side, so Cabera should approach the defusing that way.

As she works, Horatio tells her: "He used silicon gel, sanded and buffed with an electrostatic cloth...You need to stop when you feel the pressure ease up, and before you hit empty space." Right then, sand starts pouring out of the piping and Cabera figures out that the bomb is a hoax, and says she's bringing the victim out. Horatio gets nervous because he's worried about a secondary device. Cabera removes Maura from the crime scene anyway.

Horatio follows her out and then sort of pouts and paces oustside the house. As he's doing so, he notices a little boy on the bicycle with a package in the basket.

Megan sees him and mocks him for thinking that the bomber is a little boy but Horatio is not listening. He walks over to talk to the boy and then puts down a metal box that Bill had handed him. We find out the kid's name is Connor and that he got the bike from a stranger. This stranger said he could have the bike if he delivered a package. . Connor had instructions to wait for a "friend" right outside the bomb site and to give him the package. Horatio then commands Connor to get off the bike, "very slowly...in slow motion" and tells him to walk to Cabera and Megan.

While the robot is busy neutralizing the bomb, Megan combs Connor's hair to see if the bomber left any DNA behind. She finds a wavy, light-colored hair, but there is no skin tag so she can't get DNA out of it. . Meanwhile, Horatio has figured out that the bomb was a decoy and the bomber is after the bomb squad.

The bomb is analyzed and it is discovered that is houses traces of chlordane, an insecticide banned in the U.S., but used in coffee-growing countries. As this evidence is processed, Megan comes in and reveals that the hair actually came from a wig. Calleigh remembers that french lace is often found in wigs.

They all go back to the impound warehouse and a uniform hands them Barigner's file. AS it turns out, Horatio knows him. Horatio then puts on his exposition hat so we can figure out what the motivation was: "1998 was a raw deal for you when that bomb blew, wasn't it? You could have beaten that timer." Barenger says, "I would have, if I hadn't had Al screaming in my ear." Horatio continues "Al made a big mistake with you, Charlie. He underestimated you, didn't he? But now you're going to show them. You picked victims to mislead the squad, made them think they were dealing with Colombian bomb ransomers, but all the while, you were setting them up. And that last device? A work of art, Charlie. Collapsing parallel circuits. Michelangelo would have been envious."

The episode ends with Megan admitting that Horatio was right.

Wet Foot/Dry foot

A fishing boat drifts in the water and a man at the prow listens to the radio, and learns of a squall that happened the previous night. While the radio drones on, three other men sit in chairs on the deck, drinking beer. One man checks his watch and comments "I'm not working on my tan here." A man in an orange shirt and a blue baseball cap and black sunglasses throws the chum in the water. Moments later, the line jiggles furiously and we can see that the chum has attracted a shark.

Eventually the shark is pulled aboard and one of the men guts him/her. As he completes the incision, and opens up the shark, a severed human arm emerges from its insides.

The next scene is of Megan taking pictures of the arm as Horatio muses, "You find human body parts in a shark -- is that murder?" "It is when we're looking for lead," Megan replies.

Horatio breaks it to the fisherman that the shark is now the property of the Miami/Dade crime lab, and so are the nautical maps. When he protests, Horatio says, "You get a pass on your illegal GPS unit."

At the morgue, we learn that the arm is attached to part of a torso and the whole thing weighs 28 lbs and change. Alexx tells Horatio the body part in question has gynecomastia -- A.K.A. an enlarged breast which is usually caused by an imbalance in androgen and estrogen hormone levels in a man. Alexx points out that the gynecomastia introduces some gender ambiguity—in this case, there's no armpit hair, but pronounced hair on the knuckles. Alex then tells Horatio that she sees "Stippling and some GSR inside the wound. The shot was fired at close range...Dermal ecchymosis around the teeth marks. Capillaries inside the deltoid muscle are hemorrhagic. Blood was circulating at the time of the injury." Alexx pulls out a bullet, and Horatio demands a close-up of a tattoo on the arm. Megan does what he asks.

The tattoo is of the Cuban flag, upside down, with a fish symbol in the middle. Delko notes that an upside down flag is a mayday signal, and points out that Catholic leaders in Cuba also adopted the fish symbol for the anti-Castro rebellion. This could mean that the victim was a political prisoner.

As Speedle explains to Megan and Horatio, "He was from Cuba, and he was making a freedom run...based on where the shark was caught, and simple geography, it's a straight shot from Mantanzas or Villa Clara to Miami. You know what that means? Elian." Cut to Calleigh examining the bullet, and we learn that the bullet was from a .45

Speedle and Delko track down a friend in the coast guard and ask if he's seen anything suspicious lately. Next scene, they are aboard the Luna Nueva. Speedle finds tracks in the sand, and sees that the boat is missing its hull identification number. Speedle's supremely uninterested, as he's taking super-duper close-ups of the tire tracks.

Inside, they find a rosary and an empty asthma inhaler. Inside the main cabin, Delko finds a waterlogged note Speedle digs a spent bullet out of the boat's side. Delko picks up a mattress and notes a lot of blood. He swabs and bags it.

Back at the lab, Calleigh's compares the bullet Speedle brought her to the bullet from the torso. Both are .45 caliber, classic copper-jacketed, six lands and grooves, with a left-hand twist. Then Megan walks in and breaks the news that the blood on the boat matches the arm, and the victim was male.

In the next shot, the boat has been moved to some sort of hangar. Speedle is trying to figure out the ship's serial number, and Delko notes that the boat looks as though it went through Hurricane. Horatio notes that the boat has enough horsepower in it to have outrun Andrew Horatio, apparently, has thought of this too and says: "Maybe we're running at night. Never saw the squall coming." They poke around the ship more and determine that the ship had a secret compartment. In said compartment, there is beam glazed with cocaine. "This is pure snow! Do you have any idea what the street value of this secret compartment is?" Delko screams. They take a sample and bag it for evidence.

In the next scene, Speedle has managed to use Photoshop to the boat's serial number (19993187672). The boat is registered to one Captain Robert Morton. Megan instructs Speedle to watch security footage for the past few days. Speedle is concerned that Megan is undermining Horatio. She sidesteps the question and is able to have an excuse to leave him to do her bidding when her cell rings

Megan appears at the scene of another crime—a woman who washed up on the shore in an inner tube. Alexx is sitting on the side of a life raft and snapping photographs. Horatio looks at the raft and says "Cyrillic lettering. The Russians have been forever dumping their second-rate surplus on their island friends." Alexx tells everyone, "This girl's been shot in the leg. Very close to the femoral artery. Bled out. There is no exit wound, and that there is a tourniquet tied above the wound. There's no evidence of sunburn or exposure. They deduce that she was on the Luna Nueva with the person whose arm showed up in the shark. Megan notices her scapular, which says: "the Virgin of Charity," the patron saint of Cuba. Megan inspects it and says "Tonal variations, there's only one or two guys in Little Havana who do this bulino work."

In the following scene, Horatio paces and looks very thoughtful, as usual, and says: "Wet foot, dry foot. All a Cuban immigrant has to do is touch U.S. soil and they're here. Unless, of course, the Coast Guard picks you up out there, on the water, and sends you back to Fidel." So if she'd made it to dry land, she'd have gone through 72 hours of processing and walked with a green card.

Next, Horatio and Megan cruise around Little Havana and watch the old men playing dominos. They find an imposing looking older man and Horatio greets him. He says, "Basilio, bodies are washing up on shore." Basilio doesn't really think this is news: "They wash up all the time. The government doesn't care about a balsero." Horatio then whips out the Caridad del Cobre medallion, and Megan tells him that the balsera was wearing it. Basilio asks, "What's so special about this girl?" and Horatio replies, "She was shot to death."

This motivates Basilio a little, and he takes them to a house to pay a visit to people who may be connected in some way with the crimes. Horatio shows the medallion to the man of the house. He and his wife inspect it up close, and then look upset. The man says "The price of freedom for Cuban children is high. But worth it." We learn that this is a quote by Ramon Grau who spent two decades in Castro's prisons for arranging the passage for thousands of Cuban kids to the States. Horatio says, "You're one of Ramon's kids." The man nods. We catch a glimpse of the man's nephew, Pedro, in the house. Horatio asks to speak with him but is reminded that his five minutes are up.

Undeterred, Megan corners the wife and tells her that she too is grieving over losing her husband, and can she please help them find the people that killed this girl? The woman pauses and tells her the dead girl's name was Elena, and she is Pedro's sister. Basilio has had enough, reminds Horatio and Megan that the family is grieving, and hustles them out. Megan protests, "We need to speak to that boy...And we'll get a warrant if we have to."

When he gets back to CSI central, Horatio asks Speedle how they're coming along with the note; Megan tells Horatio, "I pulled Speedle off the note for the surveillance footage. My call, not his." Horatio tells Speedle to finish the footage, then do the note.

Alexx then tells Horatio that Elena's wound shows evidence of gunshot residue and stippling, and the wound tract shows traces of a synthetic fabric that she has been unable to connect to Elena's clothing. She also had significant levels of albuterol in her system. Horatio says, "She was asthmatic. We found an inhaler on the boat." Alexx continues, "My guess? Bronchospasms triggered by some kind of stress. Her heart went into dysrhythmia -- a condition that doesn't go well with a severed femoral. And that tourniquet didn't buy her a lot of time."

In the next scene, we see Megan taking DNA samples, and then telling Horatio that somebody else—not Elena-- tied that tourniquet." Meanwhile, Delko is trying to stay at Calleigh's house that night—which she eventually agrees to—and then tells him to check out the bullets. The bullet in Elena DeSoto's leg matches the bullet in the dismembered arm, and the shell they dug out of the wall of the boat. As Delko is about to leave, Calleigh asks, "Did your parents make that journey?" Delko stops in the door and smiles again as he replies, "Actually, we all did...I was in my mother's belly."

Then Delko visits Speedle who is watching security tapes in real time and going nuts doing so. He says to Delko-- "You see that rental truck there? The one next to the Luna Nueva slip? It's been parked there for six hours and 23 minutes. You see the driver? Not a cup of coffee, doesn't have to take a leak, nothing." Speedle reminds him that the boat can hold 500 kilos of blow—Horatio appears and says, "Five hundred reasons, [to wait around] gentlemen. Speed, get me in closer. Zoom in on those back tires. Now does that tire look bald to you, or what?" They break to go find a big white truck with a bald tire.

After this scene, Megan pays Horatio a visit. We learn that the material in Elena's wound tract is the synthetic material olefin, which is what dismembered arm guy was wearing. Horatio thinks through it and says:"John Doe was shot at point-blank range, the bullet penetrated his shirt, and some of the material from his shirt was sucked back into the barrel. That means the next round fired would carry that material in Elena's thigh, right?" They decide they now have enough evidence to talk to Pedro.

In Little Havana, a pissed off mob gathers as Pedro is served. Megan pokes around and finds some hair on a pillow; Horatio dusts a doorknob for prints, then notes the Colt .45 in the vacuum cleaner bag.

In the next scene, we learn that the captain of the boat and the rental truck were both at Miami International Airport, but are now in custody. Inside is a smear of blood that Delko swabs. Meanwhile, Calleigh's confirming that Pedro's in possession of a gun that shot a lot of bullets into people that are now in the Miami morgue.

Speedle is now checking out waterlogged note and explains, "The software digitizes the diluted pattern, and the algorithm extrapolates a reversal probability, estimating an image of the original writing." The writing originally read, "NM 28-30." This means nothing to either of them.

Horatio heads out to the hangar where the boat is being stored and he and Megan wander around. Megan has learned from examining the personal effects in the boat that there were twelve people aboard. Horatio adds, "What we do know is about is Captain Bob, Pedro, Elena, Doe, and an unidentified female gunshot victim. Horatio figures that huge swells and water in the fish hold would have panicked the captain and he would have had to make a quick decision: the passengers or the drugs. He chose the drugs and made the passengers jump out during the storm.

In questioning, the captain says he was blindsided by a storm and had to ditch the boat south of Matheson Hammock. Horatio tells us that it's a crime in Florida to build a secret compartment in a boat or a car. He asks for a lawyer.

We learn in the next scene that Basilio tried to arrange passage for the now-dead Elena and is trying to make amends. Horatio begins to lay out the evidence for Pedro: "The gun in your room ties you to two murders...we also have skin cells on a tourniquet you used...allegedly used to save your sister's life. Now, are you going to rebut everything I'm saying?" He shows Pedro the medallion and continues with "Pedro, habla me. You know what that is, don't you?...Now, it was never door-to-door service. The way it works is, you get dropped off as soon as you see the lights of Miami, but that night, there was a storm, wasn't there, and the captain's boat was taking on water. He took out a gun, and ordered everybody off. You refused, and he started shooting." Diaz, Pedro's lawyer, interrupts and says, "I am taking my client out of this room until there's a formal investigation in place." Horatio goes on nonetheless: "Whatever you want. Pedro, I know that you tried to save your sister's life...I know you took the rope out of the inner tube and made a tourniquet, but it didn't work and she bled to death before she got ashore, isn't that true." Pedro shot Elena, because if a Cuban refugee is wounded, the Coast Guard has to take them ashore for medical treatment and they can then begin the process of getting a green card. Pedro was afraid that Elena wouldn't be able to swim to shore, so he shot her in the leg, then began swimming to Miami.

We wrap up (finally) and learn that Pedro will be getting citizenship upon testifying. Megan then reports that the code says new moon, twenty-eighth to the thirtieth, end of the month.

CSI Miami: Season One

Just One Kiss

A woman and a man walk the beach together at night, enjoying Fabinger champagne and talking. They start to kiss, and as the intensity of their kiss builds, the man is struck down. The woman screams and there are rapid-fire shots and images: she is pinned down, he is beaten.

A jogger find the victims at 6:15 -- the dead man, and the live woman, Jane Renshaw—and of course, Megan and Horatio are at the scene. We find out that Jane, now at the hospital, is from Iowa, and she was "beat to hell, unconscious and half-drowned." Horatio looks at the footprints in the sand and decides that the man had been running from the scene, or at least trying to.

Alexx arrives and tells everyone: "Sustained blunt force trauma to the head. Multiple blows, based on the blood. Liver temperature is 87.2. Cause of death is jugular. Not a knife, though. A more irregular object. Bled out." There is a burn mark on his cheek, and he died at around midnight. They collect sample hairs from the lifeguard station. The hair is blonde, just like Jane's, and they opine that Jane and her now-late suitor had a blanket and a spot by the lifeguard station before they were assaulted. Horatio muses, "The guy tries to escape. Half-dead, scared out of his mind, he runs and someone catches up to him over here. So that makes these the last footsteps of his life." Megan's phone rings, and she learns that Jane's rape kit has been taken, and she's ready to be interviewed.

After a scene wherein the rest of the crew sifts the sand for evidence and complains about its abundance, Megan's talking to the Sexual Trauma Nurse: "Recovered what looks like some semen. Tears on the lower part of her vagina -- six, seven, and eight o'clock. Also a grade three concussion...She got antsy when I tried to administer an oral swab." She also doesn't remember the last twelve hours. Megan nods and says: "Sense memory. She's repressing." The nurse nods, whispering, "She's right on the edge."

Megan approaches her and Jane says, "They said I was attacked. They won't tell me if my boyfriend Paul is okay. Paul Varnette." Megan skates right over that last comment and says, "We have evidence of a sexual assault. If we're going to find the person who did this to you, I'm going to need your help. The more evidence we collect from you, the better chance of catching him." Megan asks for permission to conduct a more detailed examination, and Jane agrees.

After a really drawn out scene that establishes an ongoing level of tension between Calleigh and Delko, we move to the morgue. Alexx notes that there's a piece of glass in the neck wound. She also says that the victim may have been a bartender. Why? "Lime peel under his fingernails. And this rash is occupational dermatosis. You can get it from squeezing a lot of lemons or limes in direct sunlight." But Jane said her boyfriend was a CPA?...They then realize that the corpse before them is not Paul Varnette. Horatio decides to pay a visit to Jane's hotel room at the Agramonte Hotel.

There is a knock at the door and Paul Varnette opens it. "What's going on?" Horatio says slowly, "Well, Paul, your girlfriend Jane is in the hospital, the guy she was with last night is dead, and you look like you've been up all night -- so why don't you tell me?"

We go to commercial and then when we return, Horatio is looking through Paul's digital camera. Paul looks nervous. He says the last time he saw Jane was at: "Maybe eleven. We were at a party, and I passed out. I woke up at the guest house an hour ago." He is unnerved even more when Horatio takes his Cuban cigars into evidence. Paul stammers, "I don't understand." And Horatio responds: "It's not important that you do." Megan asks Paul how he got the abrasions on his knuckles and the best Paul can do is: "I was drunk. The Hamiltons throw a good party." We learn that the Hamiltons are "governors, senators, and war heros. Paul went to business school at Vanderbilt with Tyler Hamilton.

Horatio whips out pictures of the dead bartender, and instead of saying if he does or does not know the guy, Paul says: "Look, I haven't done anything. I never saw this guy, and I never hurt Jane." Megan says "Then you wouldn't mind giving us a DNA sample to rule you out." Paul cautions her that he and Jane had sex before the party, but sure, she can take a sample. He augments this with: "We were playing around, and things got kind of rough."

Later, Calleigh tells Horatio that she found something on the beach: a nosepiece with blood on it. As they walk to the Hamilton abode, Calleigh says, "I'm surprised the Hamiltons are still here; usually they're in Vermont this time of year. It's almost peak foliage."

Horatio sends Delko off to look around the property, and goes inside with Calleigh. A preppy man in expensive clothing greets Horatio, and then they get down to business. Horatio tells him he believes the victims were at his party. The man passes the buck to his nephew Tyler, and says that he was asleep; it was Tyler's party.

Horatio and Tyler then chat on the lawn. Tyler claims to be shocked that Jane was assaulted, and backs up Paul's alibi.

Horatio then asks if he can check out the guest house, which would exonerate Paul sooner rather than later. Mr. Hamilton reminds Horatio that he'll need a warrant. Calleigh, meanwhile, sees a bottle of champagne on a table and notes that the glass is very similar to the glass found at the crime scene. Mr. Hamilton notices her noticing the champagne bottle and says "Every house on this beach serves that kind of champagne and every liquor store sells it. Look, if I let you take it, then the tabloids will be calling this a raid, and I won't put my family through that." They are escorted out.

Horatio goes to his staff for updates. Delko has the name of a bartender named Estevan Ordonez. He apparently left early the night before and still has not returned to collect his tips.

At the lab, Speedle manages to piece together a large chunk of the champagne bottle. As luck would have it, there's an intact print at the base of the bottle. He then walks into a lab and says, "Guess whose prints were on that busted bottle we found at the beach? Paul Varnette." Megan is not impressed. So he continues: "Champagne bottle's the murder weapon. I tested it." The corpse, as it turns out, was positively ID'd as missing bartendar Ordonez, and the bottle matches a piece pulled out of his neck. Megan muses "So Paul catches his girl with Estevan." Speedle continues

"Offs the guy, assaults the girl." Megan points out that it's going to be hard to prove that it was indeed rape since they had consensual sex earlier that night." Also, there's the matter of the retainer from the inside of Jane's mouth. Megan found skin on the inside of the screw. She describes it: "Thin epidermis, lots of blood vessels, and the sebaceous glands are separate from the hair follicles. We're talking penis tore off."

Megan tells Horatio about this. He says "I compared the burn residue on the male victim's face to the tobacco in Paul's cigar." The cigars came from the same soil and are therefore probably the same brand. He continues "So Paul kills Estevan, puts his cigar out on his face for that personal touch for stealing his girl, staggers back to the guest house and sleeps the whole thing off." Megan replies, "One problem: I just ran the penile tissue from Jane's retainer...It's not a match." Horatio counters, "But his prints are on the murder weapon." Megan suggests, "Maybe he didn't do this alone. Maybe he did the killing --" "While somebody else assaulted the girlfriend," Horatio finishes.

In the next scene, Megan and Horatio interrogate Paul. Horatio notes that in all of the digital photos, Paul is wearing a watch he purchased at the airport, but now he's wearing a new, nice, very expensive watch. Horatio points out that this watch is a little out of Paul's price range and in comes Ryan Cutler, on retainer to the Hamiltons and taking care of Paul. Horatio continues pressing about the watch, and Paul says that it's kind of a gift. Paul says that this guy was all "'Just one kiss. Just one kiss.' That's all he kept saying." "Who?" Megan presses. Paul says, "Tyler Hamilton." And the lawyer runs like a fire was lit under his ass.

In flashback cam, we see Tyler pressing for a kiss. Not Paul's kiss; Jane's. Tyler keeps after Paul, asking him to sell his girlfriend into sexual slavery for $13,000, and eventually Paul agrees. In real time Paul says, "She was upset...I told her I was sorry, I grabbed a bottle of champagne, and said 'let's go.'" Jane didn't think it was a good idea to leave with a guy who tried to pimp her out without asking her first, grabbed the champagne bottle, and walked off. Pouting because his "I'm sorry" didn't go over well, he didn't follow her. Horatio tells him "Had you not traded her, none of this would have happened, but that's the past...I need to take a look at that watch. If you want me to buy your story, I need to look at that watch."

Megan swabs the watch, processes it, and says, "Paul was telling the truth. Found three sets of male DNA on this watch." Horatio tells her, "Separate out Paul, then cross-reference the unknowns with Jane's retainer. Can you do that?"

Back at the Hamilton House, Mr. Hamilton returns from a drive to find Horatio's humvee in the driveway. Horatio says, "I'm here for a DNA sample." Mr. Hamilton says "We have been through this, Horatio." Horatio replies, "Yes, back when I was a green CSI and driver's side airbags were standard issue. Lucky for you, though not so lucky for the young girl you had in the car."

Mr Hamilton does not take this well. He says: "And I told you, I prayed by the side of the road before you came along to help me." Horatio replies, "You know what I haven't forgotten? That chemical burn on your arm from the airbag, and your watch imprint. I haven't forgotten those things either." Horatio show him a picture of the watch. Mr. Hamilton says he gave the watch to Tyler a few months ago. I can only imagine whether he'd be pleased to learn how Tyler got rid of it. Horatio says, "There are skin cells embedded in the band...Did you know your entire genetic code is stored in a single cell? In this case, I have the DNA of two males, one of which forced Jane Renshaw to have oral sex, and the other one is a close relative. Which one are you?" Mr. Hamilton doesn't answer.

In questioning, Tyler says: "I was with her on the beach. In a sexual way, you know?" Horatio asks why Tyler didn't feel that this was relevant until now. Tyler responds: "Paul's my friend. Besides, once I hit that mousetrap in her jaw, it was pretty much over." Tyler says he left Jane on the beach went back to the guesthouse. Horatio asks for Tyler's clothes; Mr. Hamilton says "He's already admitted to a consensual act, Horatio. Let it go." Horatio reminds him that a man has been murdered. Mr. Hamilton plays the probity card and says "Yes, but the girl is the one who will pay. The press will eat her alive. Protect her." Horatio snarks, "Are *you* suggesting that I protect a woman? That's rich."

Delko and Calleigh, meanwhile, have found a dock adjacent to the Hamilton house that is public property; they will begin their search there. Horatio finds some blood drops that have somehow remained preserved. After the blood is processed, Megan tells him , "The blood you found belongs to Estevan Ordoñez. Of course, we can't tell if it's from him, or someone with his blood on him." Never mind; they still have enough evidence for a warrant. They get to the guest house and it's too late; the Hamiltons are having it destroyed. It is now a pile of rubble.

Undeterred, the CSI's suit up to pick through the wreckage. Calleigh finds a scrap of fabric, and Megan approaches

Tyler with a swab and tells him, "Open wide. Relax -- I won't jam it in too hard." Horatio pokes around and finds Cuban cigars that match the sample taken from Ordoñez's face and from Paul's cigar. Calleigh finds yet another useful item—a zipper.

At the lab they learn, "Zippers from a guy's warm-up jacket, size medium, manufactured by FUBU." There are pictures of Tyler in the jacket -- and isolated fragments of glass in the zipper teeth. The glass density matches the murder weapon; Horatio muses, "Tyler clobbers the guy, and glass rains down on his jacket." Megan confirms that the cigar has Tyler's saliva and some beach sand embedded in it. Horatio suggests, "Let's go talk to the young Mr. Hamilton."

Horatio and Megan confront Tyler in the interrogation tank. He admits nothing and looks bored and annoyed. They are interrupted when Calleigh knocks. She says "Tyler Hamilton doesn't wear glasses." She elaborates: she had DNA check the nosepiece (oohhh from a pair of glasses) three times, and it had Ordoñez's blood on it, direct spatter, medium force. Megan says helpfully, "The only way you get spatter on a nosepiece is to be there when the murder's happening." Calleigh says, "I know, but Tyler Hamilton doesn't wear glasses, so it can't be Tyler's nosepiece." Well the elder Mr. Hamilton does.

Now it's Mr. Hamilton's turn in the tank. He reluctantly hands over his glasses. What, he only has the one pair? Finally, the pieces are put together. Mr. Hamilton was alerted to trouble when he heard a scream on the beach. When he arrived, Jane was in the water and Tyler was fighting Ordoñez. Tyler became distracted when he saw his uncle, giving Ordonez the perfect opportunity to run and scream. Mistaking Jane for dead rather than passed out, he ran down the beach screeching "Somebody help me! There's been a murder!" Mr. Hamilton panicked, and to prevent further sullying of the family name, killed Ordonez.

In the next scene, Megan is with Jane at her hotel, and offers to walk Jane down to her taxi. Jane checks the room to make sure she didn't leave anything in walks her boyfriend/pimp Paul. Paul asks Jane, "Can I talk to you, please?" Jane remains tight lipped and walk out. He says to Megan, "I had no idea Tyler was going to hurt her. She has to know that. I love her." Megan says: "If you loved her, you wouldn't have traded her for a watch."

And in the final scene, Megan and Horatio eat lunch and he tells her about his past connection to Mr. Hamilton: "July 25, 1987. I found Drake Hamilton's car by the side of the road after a terrible accident. Girl in the front seat dead.

No Drake. Went up to the Hamilton residence, where I was received like a diplomat -- glad-handing, promises, blah-blah-blah, 'Drake will be right down.' Well, he did come down, four hours later, with three attorneys in tow, and a story about how he lent the girl the car. So with no clothes at the scene, a solid alibi and a mysterious chemical burn on his forearm, we had nothing. No charges were ever filed. He walked. No investigation. M.E. later told me, the girl bled out, and that all he had to do was call 911 from the road and she would have lived." Megan points out, "Horatio, you got him now."

Ashes to Ashes

At a church in Miami, Father Carlos is found dead and in a pool of blood, five minutes before he was supposed to conduct Sunday mass.

The next scene is of Horatio, greeting Detective Sevilla and Megan at the church. Megan puts on her Captain Exposition hat and tells her, "Body was found at 7:40 this morning by vic's housekeeper. She checked in on him when he didn't show up for mass." She has been interviewed already, and the last time she saw the priest was 8:15 PM the night before.

The three enter the priest's apartment. There are conveniently and obviously placed clues scattered hither and yon: bloody footprints, shell casings in the wall, blood on the wall below the embedded shell casings, prints on the coffee table.

After the credits roll, Alexx the coroner rolls the body over and we see that the priest has a tattoo on his bicep. She takes his temperature and announces that killed between 9 PM and midnight. There is a possible entrance wound, back of his neck, in the thigh, and to the shoulder. Horatio leaves Megan, CAlleigh, and Alexx at the scene, and then heads to another case.

After he leaves, Megan says: "Three possible shots and only two casings. Are we missing one?" Speedle shows her the two separate shoeprints that indicate the wearer had worn down the left sole of their shoe much more dramatically than the right. The team begins brainstorming: there's no sign of break-in; there are two glasses, but the one without alcohol has a lip-print that's probably the result of chapstick. Meanwhile, Alexx is pulling a condom out of Father Carlos's pocket,

Over at the B plot, Horatio is meeting Delko on the edge of a ravine in which an SUV has rolled to a rest. The car has been stripped, and was reported stolen two weeks ago in Georgia. Horatio says, "We've got a female driver, H. She's dead." As Horatio and Delko make their way down the ravine, they discern that the gas tank punctured, and sparks set it off on impact. The woman at the helm of the car, as it turns out, looks burnt to a crisp. Delko immediately finds a charred Cognac label There's no ID -- the purse found near the car didn't have a wallet in it. There also was a suitcase found near the car, and Horatio wonders aloud, "Now why would this poor thing travel with a suitcase and a purse and no ID?"

Back at the first scene, Megan and Speedle find blood in the holy water. Megan thinks that the killer used it to bless himself. Alexx, meanwhile, has dug a .223 slug out of the body. It's a homemade bullet cast from hot lead, it was reloaded, it was fired from a hunting rifle, and it matches the slug she dug out of the wall. The bullet, as it turns out, is a little worse for wear because it entered the body twice. The first bullet went in through the chest, exited from the shoulder, and stuck in the wall; the second shot was closer range, at the base of the neck, and exited the chest before re-entering the thigh and hitting the femur.

The glass with the lip print was marked by lip balm with SPF 45 that contained macadamia oil, commonly worn by skateboarders and surfers. As for the condom, the only prints present belong to Father Carlos. Speedle muses, "A teenage boy, a priest...we might have motive."

Next, we see a shot of Horatio learning that the burnt body has no broken bones. Alexx notes that there's soot in the woman's lungs, which indicates that she was alive during the fire. She then dumps out the stomach contents to try to draw a timeline between last meal and time of death, and finds a diamond ring in the mix.

Horatio goes to Delko and and says, "Check for her dental records and you're going to come up dry." He also learns that the tox screen indicates she had ingested 15 micrograms of Demerol, and had high levels of folic acid. Horatio concludes from this that the woman was pregnant.

Lacking enough information to positively ID the woman, they go back to the SUV. Delko notes that the fuel line is intact. Horatio finds a cork and a shard of glass in the back of the vehicle. He then examines the burns on the car and says: "See the char in the burn indicator. Look at this. It means that the origin of the fire was in the back seat and it traveled to the front seat. It also means that the fire was hot enough to melt the glass before the fire department got there." Delko, however, thinks she was doused with cognac and set on fire.

Horatio also points out that nobody steals a car, absconds with the ID of the driver, dopes up said driver, and rolls over an SUV without setting a fire him or herself rather than hope for an errant spark. Horatio says, "I think that whoever did this wanted to make sure that this mother and child were never identified again."

Cut to Alexx in the morgue, preparing to cut open the victim's uterus in hopes of extracting DNA that will be able to lead them to a father. She collects the contents of the womb in a Petri dish and hands them off to a lab tech.

At the first scene: Megan says, "We can estimate that Father Carlos laid bleeding for ten seconds before he walked to his killer." Calleigh says, "That's time for the killer to come over and shoot him." Megan notes, "But he didn't. Why? What happened in those ten seconds?" Speedle interjects: "The shoeprints found in the rectory were DVS. Who wears DVS? Skateboarders. The reason for the difference in the wear is because one foot is always on the board, staying new, and the other foot is on the ground, wearing out." Megan observes that this person is probably left handed, since he appears to ride goofy-foot. They conclude that they are looking for a teenager, probably 5'2" and left-handed. They decide to interview the altar boys. One, as it turns out, fits their profile.

The next scene is of a tract house, and Sevilla saying: "Mrs. Medina, with this warrant, do you understand we have the right to search your home and sample your son's DNA?" She does. Megan dispatches Sevilla to take the boy, Cameron, outside. As he goes, his mother tells him in Spanish, "It's all right, son. Don't worry." Megan, Calleigh, and Speedle then look for evidence inside the house. Megan finds the lip balm, Calleigh finds a rifle, Speedle finds DNA evidence, Megan finds pictures of Cameron skateboarding, and a hole in the plaster that matches the indent of a head, and some blood and hair on the edge.

Megan confronts Mrs. Medina and comments that the police have been by many times for domestic violence disputes. Mrs. Medina says, "My husband and I have had our troubles." Megan asks to speak to Mr. Medina, but his wife doesn't know where he's gone, or how long it will be till he comes back. Megan then talks to Cameron, and says, "I know you were there -- we matched your lip prints to a glass we found, and your shoe prints match the ones we took from the floor." He doesn't deny this and says "I just went to tell him, I didn't want to be an altar boy anymore." Cameron says that he was at a skateboard called Ollie Oop at the time of Father Carlos's death. Megan asks if Father Carlos ever hurt Cameron, and he says, "That's between me and God now."

Later that night, Calleigh confirms that the gunpowder she found at La Casa Medina matches the gun used to kill Father Carlos. Cameron's alibi, however, checks out.

Back at the second scene, the DNA collected from the fetus gave them nothing. The lab results for the woman's dress have come back, however, and as it turns out, it was covered in cognac, but the melted glass wasn't. The glass was covered with sulfuric acid, sugar, gasoline, and potassium chloride. Apparently, these are all ingredients for Molotov Cocktails. They also found a label on the diamond rings that was in the woman's stomach. It says: Stewart Diamonds.

Back at the first scene Calleigh says that she examined the guns found in the Medinas' shed, and the rifle that killed Father Carlos isn't among them. Calleigh wonders if the violent dad thought the priest was molesting Megan and Calleigh then head off to find Mr. Medina.

In the next scene, we find ourselves at Stewart diamonds. Horatio is holding up a blown-up picture of the ring and asking, "Do you recognize this ring?" The man sure does. That ring belonged to one Lisa Marie Valdez. Horatio says: "According to Stewart Diamonds, you and Lisa were in eleven weeks ago to purchase that ring." The man doesn't remember. He says he saw Lisa "Maybe seven, maybe eight weeks ago?" The guy claims he gave it to her to "show my appreciation for an intimate night together...Then she got obsessed and I didn't want to hurt her, so I just cut it cold turkey." Horatio says, "And now she's dead." The man replies, "Dead? How? Was it suicide?" Horatio shows him a picture of Lisa's charred remains and he recoils an says "eww."

Meanwhile, at an unmarked factory, Sevilla says they found Medina's truck, but no Medina. Sevilla, Calleigh, and Megan walk with a foreman who says "Well, he hasn't been to work since, I guess, since the end of last week." In the abandoned truck, Calleigh finds a pipe wrench covered in blood and Megan finds hair and dried blood on the steering wheel. They play show and tell and then comment on the fact that there is a rifle rack on the back of the truck cab. Sevilla asks about it; Mr. Jones says Medina is an avid shooter of crocodiles.

Back at CSI lab, Delko and Horatio examine items related to the Lisa Valdez sitiuation. These items include: a bundle of burnt roses, three pairs of shoes, a bottle of cognac, and a piece of charred rubber. Horatio cuts the rubber open, and there red folds within. Delko says it smells like strawberries. Horatio then writes down an address, and tells Delko to ask the guy behind the counter if Douglas (the man who bought the $30,000 diamond that Lisa ingested) recently bought any strawberry-scented rubber teddies. Delko reads the paper aloud. It says: "Artie's Adult Playground."

Speedle, back at plot A, tells Megan that the blood on the steering wheel of the truck belongs to Father Carlos. They also have analyzed a wrench with a strange substance on the teeth; the substance, as it turns out, was Emilio Medina's brains. Megan observes "If it was Cameron's dad that killed Father Carlos, he did it without his temporal lobe."

Back at Chez Medina, the cops have brought a bloodhound scent dog brought in to check the place. He gets excited and Megan and Calleigh head over to him. He is snuffling at a recently dug dirt patch. Under the mound of dirt is Cameron's bloodstained clothing. Just then, Megan's cell rings. It's Speedle, who finished running the tests on the hair found on the steering wheel: both of the hairs match Cameron's mother.

Delko returns from Artie's and we learn that Douglas bought rubber undergarments three days ago. Since there is no evidence, Delko and Horatio agree that Douglas walks for now, but after saying this, Horatio then goes to the computer guy Jerome and asks him for a favor. We see Jerome looking at two pictures, one of Lisa and one of Douglas.

In the next scene, we see Mrs. Medina telling Megan and Sevill, "This has nothing to do with Cameron. It was me. I killed Emilio." Megan sniffs a lie and says, "He killed your husband to protect you, didn't he? That night, you and Cameron dragged his body to the river. When Cameron needed to talk to someone about what he'd done, he went to Father Carlos." In the interrogation tank we learn that Mrs. Medina shot the priest shortly after dropping Cameron off at the skating park. She was angry that the priest had not turned in her husband for beating her, but decided it was his duty to turn her in for killing him.

And now, we go back to the second scen. Horatio is interviewing Jeffrey Douglas and saying: "Jeffrey, you lied to me about the last time you saw Lisa. You saw her just three days ago, didn't you? Did you know that she had family who thought she was still alive, Jeffrey? I was forced to tell them she was dead." The lawyer asks, "Do you have anything more than your opinion and my client's itinerary to hold him on?" Horatio lies and says "You mean, like his DNA? Jeffrey is the baby's father, so sit down." He says "See, I think this is about the baby, and you didn't want the baby to cramp your style so you force-fed Lisa Marie enough Demerol to kill her. Am I close?" The lawyer goes to leave with her, and Horatio stops them saying: "Before you go, I wanted to show you a photograph. Take a look at that. Do you know who that is? That's your daughter. This is what she would have looked like on her second birthday had you not killed her and her mother." He has conjured up a hypothetical photo based on composite features. He continues: "Know this, my friend: every year, on this child's birthday, I am going to haunt you. I am going to be all over you until I get what I need to put you in jail."

Cut to a Father Carlos's funeral, where Cameron Medina is serving as an altar boy. After the service, Cameron is met by Sevilla and a deputy. Horatio , leaves the picture of the hypothetical child at the foot of a statue of the Virgin amry.

CSI Miami: Season One

Broken

We see a person in a giant chicken costume, and another in some sort of benign looking monster costume, entertaining the attendees of a children's birthday party. A little girl asks her mother "do you see, do you see?" The mom laughs and smiles at her child, and helps her take off her sweater. The mom watches her child until distracted when a toy truck runs over her foot. She looks down and then when she looks back up to scan the crowd for her daughter, she can't find her. Eventually, someone dressed in the Zany Town uniform asks the woman what's going on, and she replies, "I can't find my baby." The employee sprints over to a control panel and gates shutter down to trap everyone inside. Ruthie's mom stands there alone as the other children rush to the gate.

Of course, the next scene is of Horatio comes strolling in to Zany Town. He hears about the victim, Ruthie Crichton, aged five, whom the paramedics just pronounced dead. Horatio says, "Nobody leaves." The detective confers with Horatio and tells him that to get from the ball pen to the restroom where Ruthie's body was found, the abductor would have to get past the arcade, a food court, and a lot of observers. Horatio then asks to be taken to Ruthie in the bathroom.

Cut to Ruthie, lying on her back in a pool of light, half-dressed. After taking a moment to look sad and pensive, Horatio begins looking around the room, noticing the recently filled trash can and the recently used sink. He leaves the bathroom and the detective says, "Fifty witnesses." Horatio corrects him: "Fifty suspects."

The credits roll and when we come back, a gaggle of crime-solving vehicles have converged and Zany Town is being decorated with crime-scene tape. Megan et al enter and Horatio says, "Welcome to the next forty-eight hours of your life, ladies and gentlemen." He then delegates to everyone. Delko's charged with securing an extended perimeter, Speedle's taking pictures, and Calleigh's looking into the surveillance system. Megan will be joining Horatio in the bathroom.

Cut to him examining the body and announcing the presence of "what appears to be glitter in the northwest quad." The camera passes over Ruthie. Her hair has been cut by someone who doesn't seem to really know a lot about hairdressing, and she is halfway out of her pink birthday party get-up and halfway into a t-shirt and pants. We also see that her hair's been inexpertly cut. Horatio says "Looks like he was disguising her, maybe to smuggle her out....Something stopped the plan, didn't it? Maybe she was screaming? Maybe the alarm system in the store."

Megan points out, "If it was the alarms, we could have a fish in the net." Horatio shakes his head and says, "Not a fish -- a shark."

Cut to Speedle, shutterbugging away. We establish that the gate at a back entrance is locked. Meanwhile, Calleigh is interviewing the manager and asks about the protocol for the gates. Through a pronounced stutter, he tells her that each employee checks a different section of the store. Calleigh says she saw stamps on people's hands. The man says, "K-k-k-k-k-k --" and Calleigh fills in the blanks with, "Kid check, kid check, you match the stamp on each child's hand to the stamp on the accompanying adult?"

Meanwhile, Delko and Speedle survey the crowd of disgruntled parents and restless children. Speedle barks: "People! Listen up! We're crime scene investigators. This is a very serious situation. We're going to need you full cooperation. I need everybody to stay with their families. Please watch your children. This is Officer Delko -- he's going to take your fingerprints. I know you're all frightened. We're going to try to get you home as fast as we can, okay?" They seem to calm down and get into a single file line as ordered.

In the bathroom, Horatio muses, "Glitter is Locard, but not from her clothes." Huh? Oh yeah. Locard's. Basically it means that the glitter is not from her outfit; it's from the killer and will link her to him/her. Speedle comes in and tells him what he's found: "Ah, automatic lock-up system, windows barred, doors gated, door's units on a keyed alarm -- it's your basic kid's playground turned into a high-security prison." He adds that there are no abandoned bags or backpack.

Horatio then tells them: "Ninety-nine percent of all violent pedophiles are male. Speed, also add glitter transfer, okay?...This guy's a pro. Prior planning, no witnesses, brought everything he needed." Megan wonders about the little boy's clothes that the killer was trying to put on Ruthie: "The clothes--they've been worn. Where would he get them? From his own family? Or, more likely, he already had them." She confirms, "Affirmative on blood." Horatio notes, "Recycled from his last victim."

Delko, meanwhile, is fingerprinting people. As he gets their prints scanned, they show up in a database. Just then, someone emerges from the crowd and tells Delko, "I'm a third-year law student at U of M. I know it's illegal for you to keep us here." Delko says, "You're right, actually. But as a human being, I think you have an obligation to cooperate like everyone else, so why don't you get back in line for me, okay?" He complies, but someone else has heard the exchange and says, "Is that true? Can I go?" Speedle places adhesive tape on the guy's chest, lifts off glitter, and says shortly, "No, you can't. You know why? Because now you're a suspect. So go ahead and get comfortable, legally."

Back in the bathroom, Horatio notices that the lock on the bathroom door is broken but he secured the area with an orange "out of order" cone. Horatio wonders aloud "How did a grown man steal a five-year-old girl from a public place and nobody noticed?" He decides to talk to the mom. He approaches her and says "Mrs. Crichton, did you guys know anyone here? Somebody she would have trusted?" She says no, and continues, "She was too good for this earth. Like an angel from Heaven. Maybe that's not even her in that room. How can you be so sure? Maybe she got out." Horatio smiles patronizingly and returns to the bathroom.

Alexx is conducting an autopsy. She says "Facial edema and petechial hemorrhages indicate raised venous pressure concurrent with asphyxia. Horatio notices how blue her lips are, and then wonders about why there are no bruises. Alexx tells him, "Ecchymosis can take up to twenty-four hours to fully develop, but yeah, we should see at least minimal erythema if she was strangled, or ruptured capillaries around her mouth if she was smothered, and I see neither." But, she says, the killer took Ruthie's underwear.

We then cut to Alexx and Horatio walking alongside a stretcher with Ruthie's body outside. The media has descended and a reporter shout out, "Is it true she was raped? Is there any indication the killer will strike again soon?" Horatio responds with "I'm not going to comment on evidence, but what I will say is this animal provided us with a mountain of evidence and we will not sleep until we've been all the way through it, because beneath that mountain lies his grave. Thank you very much." How very poetic.

Later, at CSI headquarters, Megan enters the morgue and tells Alexx "I got the results of the blue tint on her lips. Diglucose and propylene glycol, a.k.a. good old-fashioned candy." They huddle around the body again and Alexx notices a bluish blotch by Ruthie's ear.

Meanwhile, Calleigh is watching the security tapes. We see Ruthie looking at herself in the mirror and then spinning around in circles, finally turning to talk to someone who is right off-camera. Calleigh comments, "He must have surveilled the place. He knew how to stay out of sight." We then see Ruthie walking down the hall, led by the hand by someone who's still not within the camera's view. She talks into her headset to Horatio, who is retracing the killer's steps. He tells Calleigh how the perp took the road less traveled but left a footprint they could use.

Megan has studied the blotch on Ruthie's neck and concluded that it contains a usable fingerprint. When put in the database, however, there is no match. She expresses disappointment and the tech suggests that maybe they're not looking at one finger, but a cross-section of several different fingers.

Back at the scene, we find learn that there were no priors on anyone in the place, and the only reason four people have been pulled aside is because they refused to give prints. Calleigh sees the guy with the glitter in this group of four, rubs fingerprint-ridge building lotion on her hands, and then lets down her hair . She struts on over to the guy, and shakes his hand. She then drops her clipboard. He picks up her clipboard, unwittingly leaving his prints on it. Calleigh confirms his name—Brad Repkin—then walks back to Delko and gives him the clipboard.

At the back of Zany Town, Horatio and the detective are checking out the unlocked service entrance. The detective tells Horatio that anyone who wants to enter or exit needs a code to do so. The only people on shift at that time who had the code were the manager and six other employees.

They have been questioned, however, and have all checked out.

Back at CSI, Alexx tells Megan that Ruthie's fifth and six ribs on her right side were broken -- "the cracked rib punctured her lungs, her lungs fill with blood." Megan opines that Ruthie was fighting her would-be abducter, so the guy got on top of her to pin her down. Alexx notes: "Cause of death: positional asphyxiation." The tox screens come back at that moment and show that Butalbitol was in her system. Megan says sadly, "He gave her barbiturates with her candy." They also found antihistamines. Megan says "She wasn't struggling. She was convulsing." Alexx notes that antihistamines are contraindicative with butalbitol, and they decide she went into anaphylactic shock. Megan and Alexx opine that the perp wasn't trying to crush Ruthie to death, but was giving her CPR and accidentally cracked her ribs.

Meanwhile, back at Zany Town, Calleigh finds a ring and a partially eaten cotton candy cone and bags it; Horatio finds a red drinking straw and bags that. Speedlet then tells Horatio and Calleigh that there has been a new development with Repkin, who, in Speedle's has glitter on his shirt, no ID, and will not give prints. Calleigh demonstrates her scorn for due process and says "I got 'em anyway." Moments later, they receive a call from the lab and learn he's a registered sex offender. Cut to Refkin being cuffed and Horatio asks if Brad's got a car. Since he has not been read his rights, he does not know he has the right to remain silent, and leads them to the car.

Horatio tells him: "You violated your parole when you came within a hundred yards of a child. You know the rules. So shut up." They open the trunk of the car. It contains a little girl's suitcase.

Then next scene takes place in the interrogation tank where Repkin is saying, "I understand you did quite a bit of time in solitary on your first conviction." Repkin replies "That was bogus charge -- my bitch ex-wife, she ruined my life." Horatio points out that Repkin's daughter claimed that Repkin touched her inappropriately during a swimming lesson. Repkin rebuts with, "I would never hurt her." Horatio tells him "I've got footprints, I've got glitter, I've got your record, and I'm about to match a fingerprint." Repkin finally shows his hand, telling Horatio that he was planning on meeting his daughter and abducting her since it was his visiting day. Horatio replies, "Instead, you picked up a substitute, didn't you?"

Seconds later, Calleigh, who has been viewing more security tape footage, finds Horatio and tells him that Repkin was playing pocket pool just before the alarms went full blast, on camera, the whole time. So if he was on camera, he couldn't have been the culprit. "But", Horatio says "he still violated parole, and he is still going back to prison." Of course, they only know this because they violated his rights when they illegally obtained his prints, and all of the information they have on him stemmed from their illegal collection of evidence.

In the next scene we see Delko and Megan trying to figure out what the story is on the prints. The prints on the cotton candy cone match the one found on Ruthie's neck, and they all lack the natural human loops and whorls. They figure out that the perp has perhaps watched Se7en, and has been doing self-surgery on his fingertips, cutting and grafting different portions of one fingertip to another. No matter; Megan and Delko somehow cut apart the different fingertip mosaics and reconstruct them. They then discover the prints belong to one Stewart Otis.

Another day has passed and we see morning break on the horizon of Miami. Calleigh has fallen asleep at a table. She is woken when Horatio asks her to look at one of the shoe prints. She notes that all the weight in the step is in the back, which means the shoes were too big.

As Horatio leaves Calleigh to get coffee, he runs into Speedle who says gleefully "The glitter found on Ruthie is a match to the glitter found on the Zany Town vest. He must have stolen one; that's how he got in."

Once the Zany Town manager is in the interrogation room, he tells Horatio that no one with a record could work there. Horatio wants to know where the code is kept; Bernstein admits, "On my desk." Horatio sighs and says, "In plain view for everyone to see -- that's using your head."

Not only has Speedle figured out about the perp wearing the Zany Town vest to get in, he's noticed something odd in the prints: Papilio aristodemus ponceanus, also known as the swallowtail butterfly, and torchwood, found only in Biscayne National Park. Megan also then realizes that Otis Stewart has not registered his address as required by law. Horatio points out, "If he changed his prints, there's a chance he changed his name, so let's do a property search for the name Otis anywhere in or around Biscayne National Park." They find one William and Margaret Otis live at 2430 Black Creek Rd., Miami, FL. 33165. Horatio notes, "That's a quarter-mile from the park. Let's go."

They converge on the scene. At the home there is a coffee table covered in markers and papers with children's drawings, shelves of stuffed toys, a row of little girl's shoes. then, Horatio notices a shelf full of tapes and comments, "Well, he's not shy about his pornography." He then notices a toy with dust on it and concludes, "He doesn't live here." Megan says "He plays here." Meanwhile, Delko is at a number of milk cartons with a picture of a different missing child on each one. Horatio sees them and concludes, "They're not trading cards. They're headstones."

The next scene is of Alexx and the crew digging up the yard. They've found four children's bodies, and one partial body. Back at the lab, Speedle runs tests on a pair of little girl's underpants found at the scene. He has found a carbon, hydrogen, and oxygen mixture, plus some propylene glycol, sugar, and blue dye #1. Horatio notes, "Well, there's our cotton candy." The candy is in crystal form—it hasn't been spun yet—so they decide that their perp is a cotton-candy vendor.

The next scene is of Megan and Horatio at a cotton candy stand. Horatio says "Hey, Stewart. How's the cotton-candy business?" The uniforms yank Stewart Otis off to a black and white, and he is taken straight to the interrogation tank.

In the next scene, we see Alexx reading Hansel and to her two children. As she's reading, she sees that her daughter has the same type of Band-Aid on her hand as Ruthie had on hers, Alexx stops for a moment to cuddle her children, then says, "I want to talk to you guys about bad people..."

Then we see Horatio, dressed in black, watching little kids play.

CSI Miami: Season One

Breathless

There is a fancy party in Miami and the revelers are engaged in an assortment of merrymaking activities. A woman puts a shot glass between her thighs and bids a shirtless man to take the shot. The next morning, a hapless maintenance man begins to clean the area by the pool. As he tidies up, he finds a body.

Cut to Horatio and Sevilla walking towards the scene as she tells him what's going on" "We've got a looker -- twenty-two-year-old named Noel Peach. The cause of death is unknown. The camera pans over to Peach, who is lying on his back. Horatio says darkly, "I guess we can't rule out exposure."

Once we return from the credits, Alexx tells Horatio that the victim died between five and seven that morning. Alexx notes that there are no visible injuries, and Peach has a substance on his genitals which could be semen. They find a condom wrapper near by and conclude it is indeed semen. Horatio then finds a number of different hair samples and Calleigh finds an assortment of dead mosquitoes. Horatio says: "Mosquitoes who are attracted to circulating blood and carbon monoxide from breathing, which means our friend here was alive when he got bit, doesn't it?" Speedle has found a bra, and Alexx notes Peach was restrained at some point.

In the next scene, Peach's party compadres are questioned. Horatio begins with "Rough way for a night to end?" the woman replies, "I almost didn't come. This was my first time." Horatio asks "Your first time. For what?" "A cupcake party," she says. Horatio says, "A cupcake party. Care to explain that?" The woman—whose name is Nikki Olsen—tells him "Cupcake -- it's, um, kind of hard to describe. Basically, it's an environment where women are in charge. Get together and celebrate our sexuality." Horatio asks, "That celebration includes male entertainment like Noel Peach?" Nikki nods affirmatively and says, "There were quite a few male dancers there....It was harmless, really." Horatio comments "A little harmless lap dance followed by a little harmless sex." Nikkie rebuts this and says, "Cupcake isn't about having sex; it's about taking it back."

He then hunts down the hostess of the party and asks her to elaborate on the whole Cupcake thing. He says "I must admit that I find Cupcake to be an interesting concept, but I don't understand it. You don't have sex at the end of the evening. So what do you do?...Your party have rules?" Hostess laughs and says "That's the great thing about Cupcake. There are no rules." Speedle comes up and asks, "So let me get this straight: everybody gets together for sex, and then nobody has it? Everybody knows what goes on at an orgy. I mean, you can add all kinds of weird little party favors, cupcakes, weird ingredients -- an orgy's an orgy." As he's talking, Horatio sees the hostess walk outside and carefully drop rose petals into a planter.

And now for the B Plot. Delko and Megan walk down a marina and learn that two Bostonian transplants, Lisa and Mark Tupper were having an afternoon snooze when an unidentified man climbed up their yacht's ladder and dropped dead. The detective on the scene says: "Single stab wound. Pallor indicates he bled out." Megan looks around and says, "There was a lot more blood than what we're seeing." Meanwhile, Delko sees a Mag light on a counter that appears to have blood on the rim. As he looks at it he sneezes all over it. Megan comes in and he tells her of his find but leaves out the part where he contaminated the evidence. She tells him to bag it to be analyzed at the DNA lab. After she walks off, Delko realizes he blew it big-time.

At the morgue, Alexx notes that Peach's heart stopped beating and that he came up negative on the tox screen. She asks about the white substance around his mouth and Horatio says: "Six percent conchiline and ninety-two percent aragonite -- good old-fashioned ground-up pearl dust. Harmless." There are no signs he was allergic to it, and the only marks on his body are a ligature mark and a tiny oval impression on his chest. Tails on sperm indicate sex just before death, and a vaginal contribution that eluded the condom. But that's not why you're here, You think one of the women did it." He admits that he agrees. Alexx replies, "No such thing as free love." Horatio nods.

In the DNA lab, Megan tells Delko that there are no traces of blood on the knives taken from the scene. Delko adds, "Detective Puig says the rest of the Tuppers' story was confirmed. The marina owner saw just the two of them going out." Delko wonders why they would have cleaned up the blood. Megan says, "People hide things, half the time without even thinking."

Cut to the interrogation room. Lisa admits that she hit the dead guy with a flashlight after she saw a total stranger standing over her husband.

Back at the A-plot, Calleigh and Horatio are looking at her mosquitoes. Calleigh's saying, "So I asked myself: a bunch of dead, dried-out mosquitoes and conclude that since mosquitoes drink blood, something in Peach's blood must have killed them." Horatio decides, "Let's have Alexx go over the body again...looking for something lethal."

Then he and Speedle walk into an interrogation room, and Horatio says, "Ladies, someone had sex with Noel Peach just before he died, so we want to get a DNA reference swab from each of you, okay?" A woman says "That's not necessary. It was me." In the next scene, the nameless woman is claming that Peach was fine when she left him around two in the morning. Horatio asks, "What did you do with the condom you used?" The girl says they didn't use one.

At the morgue, Alexx goes over Peach's body again and finds an injection site. Nothing in his file indicates that he needed medicine delivered intravenously. Horatio connects the dots: "Poison."

On the B-plot, Alexx is telling Megan that being clocked on the head with a flashlight didn't kill the man; it was the stab wound. Interestingly, his spleen is twenty percent smaller than normal, and his heart and lungs are twenty percent bigger. Also, it turns out the stab wound has some kind of microorganism in it. Megan's mood seems much brighter.

Meanwhile, Horatio, Calleigh, and Speedle search the house where the Cupcake Party took place, and Horatio finds an injection pen, which yields fingerprints as soon as he's back in the lab.

Back at plot B they figure out what the microorganism was in the man's stab wound: barrel sponge spores, which are only found deep in the ocean. Megan muses "How is this possible? There was no excess nitrogen in this guy's system so he wasn't using compressed air." Delko replies, "I'm thinking he was a free diver. They're purists -- they dive without air tanks. The record's a hair over seven minutes. They train like crazy, condition their lungs, then hyperventilate to shut off the breathing center." As it turns out, there was an open-water diving contest that very morning over at Cranson Marina.

Megan and Delko head to the marina with Detective Puig. Within moments, the body is identified as Adam Cassidy by his brother Carson. They find a curly-haired guy who is all too happy to help them out. He says, "There were, uh, fifteen guys? We must have lost track." Megan asks whether hypoxia can cause delusions. The curly-haired guy says "not if you know your limits." Of course, free diving is about testing one's limits, so there we have it.

Megan and Delko then proceed to swab every spear and knife from that competition, and on one, they find traces of human tissue. The gun in question belongs to Ignatio Paez, so they've got a weapon and a suspect.

On the Plot A front, they have found a different sort of murder weapon: sheer purple panties. The DNA results indicate that the panties are Nikki Olsen's and there was apparently one of Noel's pubic hairs in the "intimate part of her intimates." Moreover, the clasp of the matching bra matches the indentation found on Noel's chest.

Not only that, but the print on the injector pen matches this Nikki Olsen. These pens usually contain only one dose of ephinedrine, but it is possible to double- or triple-load the pen.

In the interrogation tank, Calleigh slides a picture of the injector pen across to Nikki and she says, "It's for bee stings. I'm allergic. Arrest me." Horatio observes that there is a mark on Noel's body that matches the pen, and would she care to comment? She says, "I thought he was gonna die." As it turns out, Noel is allergic to shellfish, so the vodka, oyster juice, and pearl dust set him off. As for the underwear: Nikki has always fantasized about having a man dress up in underwear and heels for her, and asked Noel to do so. Nikki also says that Peach was dating someone else.

Shortly after the interrogation, Calleigh reports that Alexx found only one dose of ephinedrine in Peach's body. No matter; chalk found on the condom wrapper leads them to to Sophia Ananova, a twenty-four-year-old third-grade teacher.

Cut to Megan telling Mr. Paez that they found human tissue on his spear gun. He has no idea how it got there so Megan asks his permission to run a test, which he grants. Megan trains the typmanometer on Paez's ear and discovers that his eardrums are ruptured. She shouts, "You're losing your hearing, aren't you?" Apparently, this is from intense pressure when diving at great depths. We can eliminate Paez from the list of suspects, as it would be impossible for him to dive to barrel-sponge level without completely decimating his inner ears.

There is a new development in Plot B when Megan tells Delko that the DNA on the spear does not match Adam Cassidy, which means that they don't have the murder weapon. Delko finally admits "When I was processing the flashlight, I sneezed." Megan says, "You contaminated evidence. Why didn't you tell me?" Delko replies, "I wanted to, I just didn't know how."

Moving along, the next scene is of Delko, diving deep underwater to see if he can find the correct murder weapon. He finds a knife. Apparently the knife has traces of Adam Cassidy's blood on it. Given that this is Carson

Cassidy's knife, and they had a strong rivalry about diving, it's not looking so good for him.

Cut to Horatio talking to Sophia Ananova in her classroom. She gets upset and says "I don't believe this! I could lose my job." Minutes later, we find out she's carrying around condoms of the same brand as the one found on the crime scene. Sophia says, "I want to be safe! Is that a crime?" Horatio agrees that it is not, but murder is.

The interview continues in the interrogation tank. She says, "I did not have sex with that man." She is shaking and Horatio figures out that she's wearing a nicotine patch that isn't really staving off her nicotine addiction now that she's under stress.

Next, we see Horatio and Speedle staring at dead insects and Horatio saying "Nicotine is one of the most toxic of all poisons. More lethal than cyanide or cobra venom, believe it or not." Apparently, fifty milligrams of nicotine is enough to kill someone. "First, the seizures as the nicotine moves through the central nervous system, followed by paralysis. The lungs collapse, the heart stops beating. It can happen within five minutes." They determine from lab results that he did indeed die from nicotine poisoning, and go check out the body to see how it was introduced to his system. As it turns out, it was introduced through the penile tissue.

But since Sophie's box of patches is full, it's unlikely that she used a patch to kill him.

Cut to the Cupcake House gardener telling Horatio, "I keep the insecticides locked in my truck. Some of that stuff is dangerous." Just then, Speedle holds up a bottle and says, "Red Kill! Forty percent nicotine sulfide solution."

In the B-plot, Cassidy's lawyer says "Adam must have borrowed that knife. We already know he borrowed a spear gun. Look, you've got no witnesses. You've got no case." Megan asks Cassidy to take off his shirt. He's got an infected cut. Megan says, "There are your witnesses. Hundreds of them. Deepwater barrel sponge." She elaborates and says: the brothers were down around the fifty-foot mark, already in the throes of hypoxia, when a tuna went swimming by. Adam shot Carson with a spear gun, and Carson stabbed back. Carson says, "It was like a dream. My hand wasn't my hand." Megan replies, "That would be the hypoxia talking."

Meanwhile, find out Noel had called the Cupcake hostess over 107 times in one month. Horatio tells her why this is relevant: "Well, Nikki told me he was seeing someone new, and based on those records, I think it's you. But you weren't the one who wanted him. It was the other way around. Noel was obsessed with you. He pursued you, even tried to make you jealous by going off with Nikki. He wouldn't end it. So you decided to end it for him. You took the condom out of Sophia's bag, added nicotine insecticide. We found your fingerprints on a bottle in your gardener's truck. And after the party, you let Noel come to you one last time. You knew he couldn't resist."

They show her a condom that substantiates their claim. Which is weird because it seems like she would have flushed it but whatever. Horatio leans in and says, "I'm guessing that inside that thing will be nicotine, and on the outside will be your epithelial cells. You could have poisoned yourself." She says, "Why is it always about what the man wants? His decision, his orgasm, his rules." Horatio says "So you killed Noel because he wouldn't play by your rules. Is that what you're telling me?" She replies in the affirmative, and is arrested.

CSI Miami: Season One

Slaughterhouse

The episode opens with a shot of a serene suburban enclave nestled against a grassy swampy estuarian area. We see two kids carrying surfboards, gardeners tending to the landscaping, and then a toddler wandering down the street, blood on his pajamas. The EMTs and CSI vehicles swarm after the gardener noticed the bloodstains. No one knows which house she came from, and though she has no scratches on her, she was covered in blood.

The little girl cries while Horatio swabs her. They learn that the blood is human and no her own. Horatio then says, "I'm interested in that sunburn on the one side of her face. You have a sunburn on one side of your face, it means you've been walking in a straight line, doesn't it?" They figure out that she was headed north in a straight line, so they get in a car and head south.

Horatio drives for awhile and calls the lab to find out what tests have yielded. There are four, and they are all related to the little girl.

Horatio then calls Speedle, who says: "Somebody was trading the old for the new. The soil on the toddler's feet was laced with glyphosphate." Horatio says, "That's a heavy-duty grass killer. They may be resodding, so let's look for a location where they're resodding." Moments later, Delko calls back to tell Horatio that they've spotted the house with the lawn that's being resodded. Horatio pulls up and notices the open door, and Sevilla draws out her gun. Horatio gives a thumbs up to Delko in the copter, and enters the house. He gives a thumbs-up to the helicopter -- good thing Delko's got binoculars -- then heads toward the house.

There are two people dead in the foyer. One is hunched over an infant. And a woman lying on the couch seems to have lost her jaw. Horatio notices one of the bodies in the foyer is not a body—he's alive and breathing—and then asks the man, "Who did this to you?" "My son," a man answers. Horatio sees a young kid lying a few feet away, and notices the baby the boy is holding. Horatio heads into the bedroom to see a small boy, shot at the base of his head, slumped over his desk, his headphones still on. A beeping sound draws him into the kitchen. He opens the microwave and there is a bottle of baby formula inside.

In the next scene, the lone survivor is being wheeled to the hospital and the little girl is currently with Social Services.

As Delko and Calleigh arrive, Sevilla exposits: "The occupants are Jason and Stephanie Caplin. Dad's an optician at Stonybrook Mall, Mom's a stay-at-home. Four kids: the oldest is Luke, he's sixteen; Timothy's nine, and the only other victim found in a separate room. Our toddler, Erin, the only surviving child, is seventeen months. And Max...six weeks." Delko finds that the sliding glass doors were open, but no signs of forced entry, nor any other suspicious signs. Horatio says, "Okay, so everything we have is right here, and we have a happy, all-American family shotgunned to death in their own home." Speedle says, "Except for the dad and toddler." Horatio says, "Right. But if the toddler belonged home, what was the dad doing here?" Delko wonders why two school-aged children are home too. The time of death was between 11 AM and 1 PM. Perhaps they were all home for lunch? Horatio paces and Alexx notes, "Mom's wound is consistent with a self-inflicted gunshot." Calleigh points out that Jason could have pulled the trigger too.

Alexx has moved on from autopsy-ing the infant to examining Timothy, noting that there was distance between Timothy and his shooter. There was no defensive posture, probably because he was taken by surprise. Alexx blames the headphones. She also says she knows why Timothy was home from school; his temperature indicates that if he died at the same time as everyone else, he had a 103-degree fever and was home sick.
In the bedroom, Calleigh notes that this is the only bed that's not made. Calleigh notes the crib at the foot of the

bed, and Delko comments sympathetically, "Yeah, nobody's getting any sleep." In the bathroom, Delko finds a full bottle of antidepressants that was filled weeks ago. He goes to the kitchen and tells Horatio, "I don't see any sign of blood or struggle here." Horatio muses, "This place isn't a mess -- it's downright filthy. Kids will pick up after themselves, but they will not clean." They poke around the kitchen and we see that the fridge is practically empty. Horatio continues "Empty fridge, overflowing garbage. They obviously live on fast food."

Horatio says, "Well, Mom did give up the fight. Who's been taking care of the family?" Speedle tells us about the timeline he constructed: "So the toddler was here, veered away from the mother, around the father, sharp right to the brother and the infant. But here, the blood from Luke pooled around the toddler's foot." Horatio continues "So that means the toddler was over Luke when he bled out....So she was inside within minutes of the killing, but she's the only family member not shot. Why? Why was she spared?" Delko says, "She's the only girl." Speedle suggests, "Maybe she was hiding." Horatio says, "Maybe she was lucky."

Cut to the garage where Calleigh tells Horatio that Stephanie drives a wagon, but it's been a while. She continues, "So Dad goes to work, like normal. Eleven forty-five, he gets a call from Mom, and then he leaves, upset. Right? So Dad leaves his keys in the ignition, but remembers to close the garage door." They then see the gun safe and note the ammonia around the door.

Horatio tells Sevilla to take a look at the position of Stephanie's body again, observing, "She's the only victim we found at rest." Delko notes, "Females usually don't suicide by shotgun. Too messy." "Well, did you see the rest of the house?" Calleigh snarks. She then adds, "I think there was a bigger concern than this." Horatio asks, "Speed, how long do you think you're going to be here?" "All night," Speedle replies. "Keep me posted," Horatio says.

At the morgue, Alexx goes over the bodies once more "Luke, sixteen years old. Shot twice -- once in the shoulder, once at the base of the skull." Horatio suggests he was on the move, and Alexx replies. "Running only gave the buckshot pattern room to expand...newborn, a few pellets is all it took....People really don't chew, especially hungry teens." She fishes out a half-eaten French fry from Luke's stomach contents and Horatio says, "The infamous half-eaten bag of fries. So -- Luke brings home lunch, but doesn't get to eat because the killing has started." Close inspection tells us that Luke has picked up nail-biting and teeth-grinding, as well as an ulcer. Moving on to Stephanie, she's got a twenty-seven-inch reach and the rifle has a 24.5 inch barrel, so it's possible that she shot herself. The autopsy session ends when Horatio receives word that Jason Caplin just got out of surgery.

The next shot is of Jason in the hospital while Sevilla asks questions. She says, "Can you tell us anything useful? Like, who did this to you?" He says "Of course not. But have I mentioned yet that the kids were making my wife really crazy?" Sevilla says, " So did your wife threaten to do anything?" He says his wife called him at the office and he came home. Horatio wants to know why. Sevilla tells him, "She was upset. Baby wouldn't stop crying. U-turns from office to home were not unusual."

In the hall, Sevilla and Horatio figure that Stephanie was having a hard time taking care of four kids and was enlisting her husband's help on a regular basis. After deciding that there is no possibility that he shot himself in the back with a rifle, Horatio says, "Hormonal depression and long arms could get us there."

In the lab, Delko has found some long, dark hairs collected from the master bedroom where Stephanie, who has blonde hair, slept. The hair, as it turns out, belongs to a female relative. Horatio says, "Maybe Mom had more than hormones and kids to worry about, huh?"

They call in the sister for questioning. Sevilla asks her if she knew that Stephanie was seeing a psychiatrist. The sister says, "She was having a rough time. Not sleeping. And the baby -- the baby cried a lot. Colic. And she, uh...she was having a hard time." Sevilla asks, "Can you be more specific. Because, you know, baby blues are one thing, but postpartum psychosis, that's quite another." The woman now gets agitated and says "My sister was depressed! She wasn't crazy." Horatio notes, "She had medication she wasn't taking." The sister counters, "She was worried about what it would do to the baby. She was nursing." Horatio pulls out a picture of the amulet found by the baby's cradle and asks the sister about it. She says "Yeah, I gave that to her. It's a charm, to make her feel better," she replies. Sevilla snaps "How about your brother-in-law? Did you help him feel better?" Horatio cuts in with"We, um, we have evidence that you were in their bed recently." She gets even more upset and tells them she just wanted to see her sister by happy. The day of the murders, she was in Buffalo, on business. Sevilla then says rather venomously, "That doesn't explain your little trick between the sheets." Sevilla is then taken down a notch when the sister said: "I held my sister when she couldn't stop crying. When she couldn't get out of bed, much less the house. And that's a hell of a lot more than Jason did...he hid at work, day and night, leaving her alone with four kids."

Calleigh calls Horatio outside and tells him that she couldn't get any good prints from the shotgun, but she did get Timmy's prints off the baby bottle. Horatio says, "So the nine-year-old is parenting the baby while the mother is doing what?". Calleigh suggests that maybe Stephanie was opening the gun safe, as her prints were the only prints found. Horatio wonders why Stephanie didn't kill the toddler. Calleigh suggests, "Couldn't find her? I mean, she's a woman who can't function. If you can't function, you can't keep track of your children."

Cut to Speedle and Delko at the scene of the crime. Speedle notes a hallway table covered with photos of the boy. Speedle goes outside, joined soon by Delko, and they go over to a doghouse in the yard. Delko says, "They don't have a dog." Speedle says, "If they did, it didn't last." They peer inside it and find a bloody blanket, and Delko says, "I guess we know how the toddler hid."

At the lab, Calleigh and Horatio use a dummy and a shotgun to figure out if Stephanie committed suicide. After a series experiments, Calleigh says "She's either the most relaxed suicide on record, or she was taking a nap."

Minutes later, Delko summarizes the significance of the doghouse discovery by saying: "The blood on the blanket in the doghouse proves the toddler was there after someone was injured." Horatio says, "Right, but her feet were drenched with the blood of all five victims, though." Speedle rebuts: "Not until after she was hiding in the backyard. The transfer from the blanket came from one bleeder -- her mom." They figure someone carried Erin to the doghouse to save her. Both Luke and Jason have soil on their shoes. So one carried her out; one may have snapped and murdered his family.

They return to the lab to analyze the victims' clothing. Speedle discovers that the transfer stains on Luke's pants come from Stephanie. Horatio thinks about this and says "Instinctively, he picked up the toddler, thinking the killer might still be in the house. He did it after Mom was mortally wounded." Speedle tacks up Exhibit A: The Dirty Dishes, and says, "Mom and Dad aren't doing their jobs, so the son steps up to the plate." Horatio adds, "Luke tries to bring his siblings lunch and walks into a massacre....While Luke is saving the toddler, the killer goes after his next threat: Timmy." Speedle says, "Luke comes back in, tries to save the infant." Horatio continues, "But he dies trying to get the infant out the front door, and why does that happen?" Delko says, "Dad's blocking his path." Horatio thinks not and says, "Dad's been shot in the back, and his wound is not self-inflicted." Calleigh and Speedle think that Jason and Luke may have struggled over Max—the infant-- and Luke managed to shoot his father in the back. They take a look at Max's little jumper and notice three small gravitational droplets of Jason's blood, which means that Jason was hovering over the baby.

They march right over to the scene, where Jason is holding Erin. Horatio informs him that he wants to talk to Jason about the blood found on Max's jumper. Jason says, "I bled on my baby? I got shot. I guess my blood must have been everywhere." Horatio explains that the drops prove that he was standing over the baby while bleeding. So basically, Luke died protecting Max from Jason. This took place after Jason correctly guessed that Luke wouldn't shoot him while he was holding Max, Luke managed to get Max and head toward the door, where Jason shot Luke in the back a few times.

Jason goes on and on about how the burden of his family drove him mad. Horatio guesses that this will be his defense: "Two-pronged: I didn't know what I was doing, and I certainly didn't know it was wrong."

To prevent him from claming insanity, Horatio does a few more tests. There's ammonia on Jason's shirt, and a log of him calling home shortly before driving back. So he cleaned the cabinet and called Stephanie to tell her to check the cabinet so her prints would be on it.

Horatio replies, "The important thing now is that she really knows what happened." We see Erin in her aunt's arms, and the episode ends.

CSI Miami: Season One

Kill Zone

Exterior. Morning in Miami. A street scene of people hustling and bustling to go to work. The camera then lingers on a man taking pictures out on an envelope, another man scanning a newspaper, and a woman with long hair. There is a shot and the newspaper guy is down. Then the long haired woman. And finally the guy looking at photos. There's chaos, people running around screaming, a stampede, and a red balloon floats into the sky.

In the next scene, the crime scene tape is up and the reporters have descended. Calleigh and Horatio arrive and stop to survey the victims. They were all pegged with clean shots between or directly above the eyes. Calleigh asks, "So how did three people get shot in broad daylight on a busy street, and nobody sees anything?" Horatio says, "Sniper."

Alexx arrives and examines the body. She tells Horatio, "Guy in the suit, the bullet lodged in his head. That man over there, same thing." The long haired woman was also shot in the head but the bullet went through. Calleigh calls out, "I've got a divot. Victim dropped in her tracks, bullet went through her head, hit here, based on a teardrop shape, tail indicates that it traveled in this direction ..." Calleigh walks over to a wall and scoops up the bullet. She tells Horatio, "Looks like a .223."

Later when the bodies are at the real morgue, Alexx maps the trajectory of the bullets for Horatio, telling him that for the woman: "Angle is downward, into the glabella, perforated the brain, and exited through the occipital bone." So the shot went in at a 20.5 degree angle. Alexx asks what the other angles for the other victims were -- they were 20.8 and 20.1 degrees.

Over in ballistics, Calleigh has figured out that these are "Specialty bullets. Not illegal, but also not widely available." Horatio says, "It's encased in plastic to protect the bullet, making it impossible to match up the specific weapon, right?"

In the next scene, Delko is wandering onto a tour bus, where a woman in an I Love My Grandma sweatshirt has been shot in the head. Delko tells us, "She was shot at nine-fifteen when the driver stopped for a bathroom break around Second, near Langley."

Then back to the morgue, where Alexx explain how the wounds in Victim #4 are different: "Trajectory is upward, into the left temporal lobe." Horatio takes issue with this and says "You just said upward. Two-point-five degrees upward. How is that possible?" Calleigh comes by and tells them that this particular bullet was from a nine millimeter.

Horatio says, "That means we have two shooters -- one in the sky, and one on the ground." Horatio gets on the horn and tells Megan: "You and Eric are on a different case. Take the grandmother on the bus."

Horatio and CAlleigh return to the scene and set up mannequins to represent the victims, and put lasers in the heads to mark the angles of trajectory for the bullets. All the lasers are pointing to the roof of the Inter·Continental office building. Horatio says, "Six hundred and fifty yards...One shot, one kill. This guy's either military-trained or police." Calleigh adds, "Marine Corps, probably. They're the best snipers in the world."

They head to the building and Calleigh thinks aloud and says, "He would have had to disassemble the rifle and hide it in something to get it up here. Maybe it was a Winchester Model 70 or a Remington 700, I don't know. Charles Whitman disguised himself as a deliveryman to get up the Texas tower and he got up there, wheeled his guns and his ammo onto the observation deck, and killed fourteen people. He wounded thirty-one." Horatio then asks, "If I was a sniper, what is the first thing I would do?" Calleigh answers "You'd pick your spot. Prone position is best for shooting." They eventually conclude that the sniper was perched atop a maintenance entrance.

When they get there, Horatio finds a the cone-shaped deposit of gunshot residue, which was formed when the bullet exited the gun. Calleigh, meanwhile, finds a scrap of burlap and gravel glued together. Horatio says, "Know what that is? That's from a homemade urban ghillie suit. That's what Marines use in the desert as camouflage." Calleigh also notes that the shooter used a sand sock to stabilize his firearm while he shot

Back on the grandma case: Delko, Speedle, and Megan determine that the bullet dinged a mailbox on its way to killing someone's grandma. They also realize that the camera from a nearby ATM may have captured some useful footage. Calleigh reports that the tape the sniper used to fasten the door was electrical tape, and Horatio has found a pine needle of some kind on the roof.

Calleigh, as it turns out, used to date a sniper for the marines and they are on good terms so... cut to Calleigh and Horatio at her ex's rifle range. Her ex gives them this diatribe: "When it comes to shooting, you can't trust just your eyes...most people think a bullet travels in a straight line. The actual path of a bullet is arced like a rainbow. That's the first thing your sniper has to take into account. The next thing is the wind. See that tall grass fifty feet ahead? It means the wind is moving three to five miles an hour. Seventy-five feet, wind's completely different. Look at those tall reeds. Tells you the wind is going five to eight miles an hour." Horatio concludes, "So no matter where your target is, you adjust for the wind." Now that we've confirmed that projectiles indeed operate on a parabolic curve, we turn to the grandma shooting.

Sevilla and Megan question a witness they found by viewing the ATM footage named Mr. Santoya . They tell him a seventy-three-year-old grandmother was killed and it happened right near the ATM, and did he see anything? No, he sure didn't.

And now we get back to the pine needle. It comes from a plant commonly used to grow bonsai trees and is not native to America. Calleigh comments, "Our sniper has a hobby." Horatio agrees, "Yessss. And patience. It takes twenty to thirty years to grow a bonsai tree. I also found urine." Calleigh says, "Probably up there all night while waiting to take his shots." Speedle comes in, and announces, "It happened again."

Cut to the scene of the crime; Horatio, Calleigh, and Speedle are getting the inside scoop on the situation from Sevilla , who says, "He just bought a hot dog and fell over dead." Sevilla asks: "Can we place him on a building?" Calleigh replies, "Not with just one bullet, but I can approximate distance." Sevilla sighs: "So the only evidence we have are bullets we can't use, and strips of a homemade ghillie suit." Horatio seems undeterred and says "The further the evidence takes us from the crime scene, the greater the chance he'll let down his guard. And that's when we'll get him."

Megan, meanwhile, is trying to pin something on Mr. Santoya. She says,"At 9:15, Ray Santoya was at the ATM." Delko asks, "So the question is, what was he doing at 9:16 AM?" Megan asks Delko to enlarge the security camera still of Santoya at the ATM, and he notices a reflection in Santoya's sunglasses. It's a patch for the Neuvitas baseball team. Megan concludes, "He's talking to whoever's wearing that jacket." "We may have a witness," Delko says. "To both shootings," Megan replies.

At Chez Santoya, where a young man in a Nuevitas baseball jacket opens the door and asks if he can help Megan and Sevilla. Megan immediately notices the black, grainy dots littering the arm of the Nuevitas jacket and Sevilla presents her badge and says, "Miami-Dade police. Can we come in?" The boy, Gustavo Santoya, lets them in and tells them that Ray Santoya isn't home. As soon as Megan, Sevilla, and Gustavo are in the living room, Ray Santoya comes out and asks what's going on. As it turns out, Gustavo's jacket tests positive for gunshot residue. Gustavo explains, "I swear on my mother's grave, no lo sabía. I didn't know -- people were yo creí que veía al que disparava." Megan prods, "You thought you saw the sniper?" Gustavo says, "No, not the sniper." Megan asks, "Then who?" Gustavo says, "The car was full of callajeros, street kids. I thought I saw a gun -- él tenía una pistola negra -- a black gun, he was holding it, I swear to you. And I didn't see any woman in the car. Solo los quatro muchachos -- the four boys were laughing at the people dying." In flashback cam we see the gun aiming at the car, and as the bullet ricochets off the mailbox, it bounces into the tour bus. Gustavo says, "Tell her family I'm sorry. I was only trying to protect my father."

Back at the lab, Horatio and Speedle check peer into a microscope and Horatio says, "The sand on the right is..." "...is a mixture of calcifying green algae and brown Swiss cheese-looking grains, uniform in size." "Likely from erosion," Horatio says. "Beach sand," Speedle adds. He then looks at the sand which was found on the rooftop where the sniper lay, and says, "Gastropods, snails, and football-shaped rings of benthic foraminither." Horatio says, "Not homologous. I'm thinking from a quarry."

Calleigh comes in to report as well: "Based on the penetration test -- I used a gelatin block to reconstruct human tissue -- the shooter was 975 yards away. Horatio tells Calleigh that "the sand in the shooter's sand sock is coral." Calleigh concludes, "So he practices shooting in a coral quarry." Horatio pulls up a map of Miami, points out the three coral quarry locations, then pulls up a chemical analysis and narrows it down to one.

And now they're at the quarry. Horatio notices a stake with a piece of orange tape tied to it. He hands Calleigh the binoculars and they map out what happens here: the sniper lies on the platform below the grate, and uses the orange tape as a flag to judge the wind. The bullets then end up in a big pile of sand, which Horatio promptly hunts through.

While he does that, Calleigh lifts prints off the wind marker and matches them to Christopher Harwood, ex-Marine, special ops. They then go to his pad hopefully getting a search warrant first but you never know.

The apartment is Spartan and clean, decorated with bonsai trees. Calleigh concludes, Horatio then notices a cabinet filled with cards and Calleigh notes, "He's recorded every shot he's ever taken." "Or planning to. This one was dated this morning," adds Horatio. We see it and it reads at top "Sniper Data Card." Calleigh turns over the card and notices the black smudges. She and Horatio conclude that it's residue from a rooftop, and it could lead them to where he's going to be.

First they contact Speedle. The only think that he's found that links the victims is that they were all in a hurry: one came from a one-hour photo shop, and the other from a one hour cleaners. So far, that's all that binds them.

Speedle tells Horatio later, "The substance on the back of the data card was a hardcore adhesive called RT600. It was only used two years after Hurricane Andrew --" "To prevent rooftops from going airborne in case of another hurricane," Horatio finishes.

Speedle has used the smudge on the data card to narrow the possible buildings down to one. Horatio checks the lines of sight from the building. Horatio comments, "That's his line of sight, lots of people walking around." Speedle says, "Yeah, but that's got to be 800 yards away."

Delko and Speedle now roam the skies of Miami in a helicopter. Delko tells Horatio, "Okay, H, I'm in position to scramble the wind condition." Two squad cars and a police vehicle of some kind pull up. Calleigh radios Horatio to tell him she's taking the stairs. He then screams through a bullhorn "Ladies and gentlemen, there's a sniper in the vicinity. I need everybody out!" People amble away without screaming or running.

Horatio, now in the line of site says, "Listen up! This guy is one shot, one kill! If he can't make it, he's not going to take it! Eric, the wind from the chopper ruins his shot!" Calleigh checks in and tells Horatio that the SWAT team has the sniper in its sights. The sniper keeps aiming at Horatio. Two SWAT team members creep up behind him and tell him to drop the weapon. Cut to Calleigh telling Horatio, "The sniper has been apprehended. We have him in custody."

Then the sniper comes down, and as he's led past Horatio, he asks, "Don't you want to know why?" Horatio doesn't apparently, and says "You just killed four innocent people. You're evil. You enjoy death. I hope you enjoy your own."

A Horrible Mind

The scene opens with a jogger sporting a Cabrerra University wifebeater runs in the woods. Eventually she trips and falls on her face. She look sup and sees a dead, bound, naked guy hanging from a tree, and takes off in a sprint.

The body is of a dark-haired man, hands tied behind his back, strangled by the rope connecting him to the bough of the tree, wearing nothing but boxers. His body is covered with bruises and punctures and abrasions.

Calleigh and Horatio arrive, of course, and Calleigh takes pictures of a pulley, and some chains wrapped around a tree branch that seems to have been there long enough for the tree to have rust on it. Speedle bags scraps of bloodstained fabric and the remains of a Dalmatian. The deceased is Adam Metzger, cultural anthropologist, professor at the university.

Next we are at the morgue. Peering through a magnifying lens into Metzger's irises, Alexx is surprised to find retinal burns. We discover that the professor's eyelids have been glued open. Alexx moves on to the corpse's other wounds, listing nine six-inch-deep puncture wounds, eight twelve-inch contusions indicating blunt force, fourteen one- to two-inch cuts likely from a razor blade, and a series of needle marks on the soles of the feet. None of these wounds were fatal. The professor died of asphyxiation when hoisted into the tree. They conclude that he went through four to six hours of torture before dying.

In the next scene, we watch a sedan get pulled out of a canal. There are no skidmarks so Delko concludes that the car was pushed into the water. He and a diver also conclude that the car sank quickly, as the windows are wide open. They force open the trunk and we catch a glimpse of a bloated corpse. Delko exposits that three or four weeks' worth of bacterial infestation have bloated out the corpse with rancid gas. The car gets jostled a bit as it is secured to the towline, and the bloated remains explode.

In the lab, we find out that the blood on the fabric gathered in the woods doesn't match the professor, so it might be the perp's. Speedle inquires as to which area of the professor's body bore the brunt of the torture. "Scrotal sack," Horatio says.

Next, Dean Hernandez is talking about the dead professor. He says that students loved him. However, the students' parents, the professor's colleauges, and Hernandez himself thought Metzger was "a whack job." Classroom guests included white supremacists and dusky prison interrogators of indeterminate origin. The professor assigned his students to sit through "home movies of slaughter, torture, and lynchings." Horatio wonders how many students the professor had. "Thirteen," answers Hernandez.

In the following scene, Horatio informs some of the students that he will be swabbing them for DNA.

After the commercial break we learn that one of the DNA samples matches the blood found on the fabric. Ned says that he was forced to participate in a "mock lynching" in which he played the victim. During this little educational exercise, Ned's classmates tore his clothes from his body, scratching his skin with their fingernails. Ned says that Metzger set the whole thing up to demonstrate how "normal people follow social norms."

Moving right along to the home of the Professor, Horatio and Speedle enter and find a few students in the professor's dining room. As it turns out, the prof had an open-door policy, and all of his students have keys to his home. "We were all really close," a student explains.

In the professor's study, they poke around before stumbling a cabinet containing a chastity belt and an iron face mask, among other things that look like medieval torture tools. Horatio swabs them.

In the garage, Delko and Megan rifle through the car. In the corpse's clothing, Megan finds a wad of paper, a car key, and some loose change. In the trunk they find a Neil Diamond CD, and notice fingernail grooves on the trunk's interior. Just then they receive word that the guy died not from being hit on the head, but from drowning.

Calleigh, meanwhile, arrives to see if any of the prof's collection of medieval torture devices were used to torture him. Speedle pieces together the shredded documents found in the study. None of Calleigh's weapon impressions match the wounds, and the blood from the swab is from a dog.

On the Aquaman Tip, Sevilla and Delko enter a metal shop to interview one Lorenzo Castenotto, the owner of the car. Larry has little interest in discussing his car. He received closure when he got the check "from the insurance." Delko then tells him about the car key found on the corpse in Larry's trunk. They show him a picture of the corpse and he almost barfs. Delko then notices a dashboard hula girl that matches the adhesive he found on the dash of the car. Delko tries to take it but Larry refuses, wanting them to get a warrant first.

Elsewhere, Calleigh finds that the wounds on the dead Dalmation match the instruments of torture from the professor's house. She finds a doggie detector microchip on the dog, and they learn that "Fisher" the "Dalmation" was owned by one Ginny Taylor of 1021 Laurence Street.

After commercial, Ginny Taylor, one of the professors students, is dismayed that the professor kidnapped her dog to torture and kill him. She swears up and down that the prof is brilliant and then immediately reveals that the professor once ordered her to lick his shoes. And she did..

So, on to CSI Central so the B plot can move along. Sevilla and Delko meet with the bloated corpse's former ex girlfriend. Sevilla found the ex by sorting through recent missing persons reports and matching the description of a "Doug Reid" The body. The girlfriend, Caroline, dated him deceased for three months. She got angry when he disappeared, thinking he jilted her, and tore up most of the photos of him. Luckily she has one photo, which she hands over before leaving.

Back at the morgue, Delko's eagle eye spies a pair of earplugs in Doug's ears, and notes that what remains of his clothing is a uniform from Larry's machine shop. Delko hightails it to Larry's, breaks into Doug's locker and retrieves the custom earplugs. He races back and learns that Alexx had the body cremated the day before. Delko does something complicated and improbable with a computer and matches the plugs to the ears nonetheless.

Back at plot A, CAlleigh has figured out that the vegetable fibers in the twine binding the professors hands are from Colombian bamboo. Horatio somehow matches this plant to one of the prof's guest lecturers. The guest lecturer is subsequently interrogated. and suggests they summon the gentleman for a chat.

The guest lecturer is Señor Barbosa, formerly of the Colombian secret police. Calleigh does the talkng since she speaks Spanish. She opens with asking what his relationship was to the prof and Barbosa replies, "Usted es una muy buena estudiante, señorita." "She's not a student," says Horatio. "She's a police officer, so I suggest you answer her questions before you have to answer mine." Barbosa says something in English to the tune of "we're all students at one time or another" or something like that. Horatio says "So you speak English. This is about power for someone like you? A narcissistic fantasy in which you degrade somebody until they lose their identity? Their soul?" They go through more of this back-and-forth where Horatio takes the moral high ground and we learn that he couldn't have tortured and murdered the prof because when he was in Columbia, he had the flexor tendons in his hand severed with a machete.

At the B- plot: the bloated corpse is indeed Doug. The wad of paper was a deposit slip for Larry's checking account. Larry admits to the insurance fraud, but insists that he had nothing to do with Doug's death,. On the night Doug took care of the car, Larry was at the dog track and even has the credit card receipts to prove it.

At the A plot: Speedle has pieced together a few of the shredded documents found at the house of the Prof. One says: "The experiments with the dog exceeded my expectations. Standing under the tree taking notes, I could feel my assistant breaking." The CSI team decide that one of the thirteen students must also be his assistant, and as such must have left fingerprints on the professor's stuff—specifically, his computer. As it turns out there are no usable prints on the computer.

In the office, however, they find a letter opener, a tape dispenser, a stapler, a pencil sharpener, a box of silver push pins, and a staple remover. Speedle points out the impression of Whack Job's face on the Xerox machine's document glass, explaining the retinal burns. The final piece of evidence recovered is a bit of cotton that was snagged on the copier..

Cut to one of the students opening her door to find Speedle with a warrant for her taser.

At the B plot, Megan emerges from wherever she's been, and she and Delko figure out what happened to Doug: After parking Larry's car on the embankment in the rain, opening the windows, and setting the emergency brake, Doug attempted to get the Neil Diamond CD from the trunk. Doug slipped, cracked his head, and drowned when the trunk closed and the car sank in the canal.

As for the professor: he broke Teresa, his student, as part of some kind of experiment. At some point, he branded her forearms, and at another, he killed the dog. Then she snaps. She tasers him in the crotch; stabs him with the letter opener; glues his eyelids open; blinds him with the copier; marches him to the woods, and leaves him on the pulley so he can die.

And there we have it.

Camp Fear

A school bus drives down a country road, stopping to drop off a group of teenagers wielding orange trash bags. Two girls decide that smoking is vastly preferable to picking up trash, and sneak off into the brush to have a cigarette. Their tee hirts, it should be noted, say "Briar Bay Baptist Church: Adopt a Highway."

They settle down for their cigs and one sees the body of a girl, wearing nothing but underpants, her eyes rolled back.. Alexx and Horatio arrive, and immediately determine that this was the site of the body dump, not the murder. Calleigh finds a tread mark and crouches down next to it. She says: "Faint tread impression, knobby tire, narrow track width. Put it all together, it spells ATV."

And her comes the B plot! Speedle and Delko are walking together, presumable to the scene of a murder, and Speedle exposits: "Delacroix says this guy's a wharf rat." Delko adds "His ex-wife came by to check up on him. Said he'd been ducking her calls for a week." They enter his silver trailer and immediately note the wretched smell. They turn over the body and determine that he was torched. Delko says, "No signs of forced entry. Probably someone he knew." "Like a pissed-off ex-wife," Speedle comments.

Delko picks up the cell phone and observes that Stango's missed a lot of calls. They decide to start by calling the missed calls.

As for the half-naked minor: the liver temp indicated that the girl died somewhere around 5 AM that morning, and her body is covered in insect bites. She also sustained blunt force trauma to the right side of her head. Horatio opines that somebody hit the girl and dumped her. Alexx mentions that there was slight vaginal tearing around the opening. Then she holds up a diaphragm aloft and says sadly, "Fifteen years old and she was planning on having sex." Horatio comments, "Well, someone was. Maybe someone who didn't get their way."

They are interrupted by a lab assistant who hands Horatio an envelope from Megan that says "PERSONAL AND CONFIDENTIAL."

While he's looking at it, we learn that although Jane Doe smelled like beer, her tox screen came up 0.0. We also learn that her blood was slow to clot, but oddly, she doesn't have any bruises. Horatio asks, "We've got no ID, no crime scene and no cause of death, right?" Alexx says, "I'll swab her nasal passages and sinus cavities."

Meanwhile, Calleigh has learned that the treadmarks are of DTP Mudgator's quad-claw design, which is standard issue on 650-series ATVs. Horatio nods and looks carefully at the laundry mark on the t-shirt the girl was wearing. Calleigh says, "Used to separate identical quantities of clothing." Horatio replies, "An invisible laundry mark, just like our Jane Doe, who's not been reported missing yet, has she?"

And now, the B-plot. Speedle watches Alexx do the autopsy. He helpfully tells her: "Partial thickness burns on the lips, tongue and oral mucosa....Stomach lining appears to be red and inflamed...Swelling of the main stem bronchii, release of edema fluid." "Meaning?" Alexx asks. "Meaning he was fried from the inside, and the heat from the burns blocked off his airway," Speedle answers. She praises him on how well he did, and says she'll get back to him re: the tox screen etc.

Elsewhere, a tech is analyzing Jane Doe's snot and finds a kind of pollen that looks a little bit like an apricot. Horatio's found the ID for the laundry mark -- Pharos Academy, a juvenile boot camp for girls in southwest Dade County.

The next scene, of course, is of Horatio and Calleigh arriving at the academy. A young lady is being forced to do pushups while a drill sergeant type person pours water on her. They are then approached by a Sergeant Cawdrey who barks: "There's been no crimes committed on this property, I can tell you that." Cawdrey looks at the autopsy photo and says that Jane's not one of his cadets. At this moment, Horatio is a tadbit distracted by the parked ATV that matches the treadmark they lifted earlier. So in the next scene, it's being taken away by a CSI truck. Cawdrey claims that only instructors have access to the ATVs— except for the a few cadets that are regarded as staff members. Horatio wants a list of those cadets. Cawdrey says "These girls are minors. I can't give you anything without parental permission." Horatio's all, "We'll get it after we inform their parents they're part of an ongoing murder investigation." They show him the laundry tag and he says it belongs to barracks 2. They go off to interview the girls and search.

There is a locker inspection, and we soon find out that Cadet Julie Morales is missing a shirt. Horatio asks her where it is, and Morales replies, "Sir, this cadet does not know, sir." Horatio shows her the photo of Jane Doe again, but Morales doesn't know her. Calleigh begins searching her locker and holds up a picture of her and a young man"Is this your boyfriend?" "No. That's my brother," she replies softly. "Eyes front, cadet!" Barreiro barks. Calleigh continues going through the locker and finds a long blond hair, the same color as Jane Doe's. "Sergeant, we're going to have to process these barracks," says Horatio.

Horatio finds a grainy patch of something on the floor and takes a sample. Chaos nearly ensues when Horatio says he'll need-- Cawdrey's belt and pants; there's a tiny blood stain on the crotch.

Back at the B-plot Speedle has found gasoline all the way down to his stomach lining. Delko says, "Someone poured gas down his throat and blew him up." The sodium indicates the presence of saltwater so they decide to go to the marina and see if he had a boat.

On the plot A front, we learn that Jane Doe is Dara Winters, and her mom just filed a missing persons report. "She was a teen model," Horatio adds.

Off to Dara's house to interview mom then. We learn she left the house around 8 PM with friends, and she was wearing a red halter top and a black miniskirt. Sevilla asks why Mrs. Winters waited so long to file the missing persons report and she says that it wasn't unusual to not see her daughter all morning, so she didn't begin to worry until afternoon. We learn that Dara was an A student who didn't allegedly do drugs or smoke, and as Mrs. Winters shares this information, Calleigh fishes under a piece of furniture and finds a collection of letters. Calleigh asks, "Did you know she had a P.O. box?" No, she did not. The letters have no return address, and they bear the signature of a "Louise".

Back in the B-plot, Delko and Speedle find the victim's little boat and from the many gas cans aboard it, Delko says: "The idiot was siphoning."

And on the A plot, the substance from the floor of the barracks was salt. Also, the pollen grains found in the ATV's air filter match the pollen grains found in Dara's nose. And, more importantly, the blood on Cawdrey's pants matches Dara's blood.

He is immediately dragged into the tank and Horatio asks: "The blood on your camouflage pants matches that of a fifteen-year-old girl you've never seen. Can you explain that?" Cawdrey says, "I'm very sorry for this girl and her family, but if she was in my camp, then she was trespassing...Last time I rode that ATV was yesterday morning. I ran it out to the chapel, then to the latrine, then back to admin. Whatever you guys are Cawdrey then willingly gives prints and a nasal swab.

In the next scene, we learn that there were two sets of prints on the diaphragm and that neither have been ID'd.

Horatio starts brainstorming on how Cawdrey got the blood on his pants. In flashback cam we see : Cawdrey riding the ATV, stopping, opening up the area in which the keys are, inadvertently getting blood on his hands as he picks up the keys, then stopping at the car, where the blood finds its way to his zipper.

As for Stango, the exploding man: he was siphoning gas with a plastic tube and his mouth. Moreover, the type of fuel he was stealing has got a low flashpoint -- you're not even supposed to store it in the sun. Also, of the last one hundred incoming calls Stango had, seventy-four came from someone named "Motor."

At the lab, Horatio and calleigh figure out where one can find the tree that was the source of the pollen in Dara's nose. They adjust for the wind, and the location of the trees, and decide that Dara took her last breath within fifty yards of the pond just inside the Pharos Academy perimeter. Sure enough, when they drag the pond, they find a black bag, a red halter top, and a black miniskirt. Calleigh comes out of the pond covered in leeches (ew) and when they use salt to get them off, they realize the salt from the barracks may have been used for the same purpose.

The leeches, they decide, explain why there's no bruising on Dara Winters. The leeches removed the surface blood and the anti-coagulant acted like a blood thinner so she never clotted. They surmise that the leeches smelled beer on her, went to work, and possibly killed her.

Horatio enters and says "So we've been going through the letters we found in Dara's room, and they appear to be written in some type of a code: 'Tell QB no more. You have to get the hell out of there.' This girl has a secret, doesn't she?" In the next scene, the girls of Barrack 2 are lined up so they can be examined for leech bites. Morales looks particularly reluctant to submit to this examination so Barreiro barks, "Double time!" Horatio says, "You heard her Louise?" she looks up, appearing to be responding to the name "Louise". She replies, "Sir, this cadet's name is Julie Morales, sir!" She also has leech marks on her calves.

Back in the B-plot, we find out that Stango was selling Motor bad gas and trying to pass it off as good gas. Motor's boat sustained damage because of the bad gas, hence the repeated calls. Delko asks about the one call on the morning of Stango's death, and Motor says, "I star-67'd him, and when he picked up, the line went dead."

Cut to 1. Horatio opening a letter from Megan in which she asks not to be contacted any more and then 2. Barreiro explaining, "I wanted to cut Julie a break. I was on bed check. I heard talking coming from number two after lights-out." Horatio asks, "And that's when you saw Dara?" Barreiro says yes. She had come to the camp cause she needed to talk and Louise was her best friend. Morales says, "I told her she had to leave immediately. I escorted her to the front gate and I left her there...I found her by the pond at 0700 morning rounds. I drove up and she was just lying there."

Calleigh asks, "Why was she running away, Julie? Did it have anything to do with you assaulting your mom? ...We talked to your parents. They told us the whole story." Morales says, "Dara was sick of the modeling. She was sick of everything. Always having to be perfect! But Queen Bitch wouldn't let her quit." Cut to a bizarre shot of Mom waving a diaphragm around and saying "You'll use this diaphragm or else, young lady!"

Over at the B plot, we see Delko and Speedle trying to figure out what happened. Basically, they go back and forth and then we see a flashback of Stango answers the phone and it ignites the gas in his stomach.

A-plot time again, and Calleigh's examining Mrs. Winters's car, and finds pollen on the seat.

Cut to Mrs. Winters in the tank. Horatio opens with: "You were out there the night Dara died, weren't you? We found a very specific airborne pollen on the headrest of your car which would put you within fifty yards of where she took her last breath. She was running away from you, wasn't she? To Julie. She would go wherever Julie was, so you drove out there to bring her back, to bring her back to everything she was running away from, right?" We see the flashback: Dara wandering along the road in a t-shirt and underwear, her mother pulling up and shouting, "What have you done to your hair?" They argue and Dara screams, "I'm going to tell! I'm going to tell everyone!" Mom peels out. Dara runs, trips, and hits her head next to a leech-filled pond. Mrs. Winters continues, "Dara was special. She was going places. Anyone could tell. But she was throwing it all away, and for what? A date at the mall? High school football on Friday nights? Some kind of average Briar Bay experience?" Horatio says, "To three quarters of the world, that sounds like a slice of heaven. She was running away from you because you made her home life hell." Mrs. Winters protests, "All I did was set up auditions. I was trying to help her to succeed."

We then, in the next scene, learn that Megan resigned. She said that work was too much of a reminder of her husband's death.

Entrance Wounds

Two people are making out in a hotel room discover a dead body under the bedspread, because it was covered with flies and the flies were loudly buzzing away.

The dead person is one Susan McCreary, booked on a string of priors for prostitution, dead from being stabbed repeatedly with a slender object. The killer also bathed the body in cardamom to mask the smell. Some toiletries and towels are missing as a result

At the B plot, CAlleigh and Sevilla arrive at the scene of an "attempted car-jacking and robbery. German tourist couple. They stopped for directions." The wife -- who's alive -- is Greta Roebling, and her husband – who is not -- is Werner. The husband ran when he heard shots and his body was left on the floor of the garage. Delko and Calleigh note blood in the car and on the garage and begin processing the scene.

Delko leans down to get a look at the body and says he's only seeing one entrance wound -- behind the ear, that exited through the mouth. They are puzzled, however, as to how a man could run if he was shot in the head. They are also puzzled about the fact that there is no bullet anywhere.

At the morgue, Alexx points out traces of adhesive on Susan's wrists and feet.. Horatio says, "So he picked her up, bound and taped her, and then he went to town." There's also no sign of sexual activity, which convinces Horatio that the killer killed for the thrill. He goes over Susan's stuff and finds a fingerprint.

Speedle too has found something: "Smear on the bedspread is mold -- a type that's not found in the bungalow." They determine that the mold may have come from a passive transfer, and that fingerprint belongs to Cole Judson, who had a prior knife assault on a woman twelve years ago.

Cut to Horatio arriving at the home of Cole Judson. Will wonders never cease. Anyway we learn that Mr. Judson has noisy and ill-behaved children, makes six figures somehow, and still rents nonetheless.

Ah. The B plot., Calleigh and Delko review the security tape. They figure that the smear on the floor came about by the shooter sliding through the blood, skidding, and using his hand to catch himself.

Shortly after they discover this, Alexx calls and tells them that they couldn't' find the bullet because it was fragmented. We do know that the bullet entered by his ear and came to rest by his throat, and see a nice visual of him spitting blood as he hides from his attacker.

At the A plot, Horatio et al are still searching the Judson home when Wendy Judson's ex husband Michael stops by to pick up the kids. After the kids are removed from earshot, the detective asks the wife "Are you aware that your husband has a record for a knife assault on another woman?" We then find out that Wendy says Cole couldn't have been off murdering anyone the night before because Cole has a weekly sales meeting -- Wednesdays until 9 PM.

In the tank, Horatio the crime fighting genius learns otherwise. He asks Cole where he was the night before and Cole says: "After work, I took a walk on the beach. It's what I do every Wednesday...I love being married, I do. And I adore those kids. I steal one night a week for myself, and I should have been honest with Wendy about needing it." Horatio nods and asks, "What about the girl you stabbed in college?" Cole says, "Oh, my God. Beth? I never hurt Beth. We were young, and we were drunk, and we were arguing, and she cut herself. I took her to the ER to get stitches, they had to file a report, suddenly she was worried about what her family would say, so she said I did it." Horatio then busts out the big guns and shows him a picture of the dead hooker, asking repeatedly if Cole knows her. The answer comes back repeatedly that he does not.

On the B train: the bullet that was recovered in the murder matches one fired in a robbery by one Malcolm Davidson, who only did a few months and is out now.

They promptly arrest him, ignoring his poor, sweet old gran who says that Malcom was with her the night of the foiled carjacking.

The next scene is of Horatio showing Speedle how you can frame someone with their own print, and explaining that this seems to have happened to Cole.

Things aren't looking too good for Malcom: a glove found at his house has Werner's DNA, Malcolm's epithelials, and lipstick on it. This lipstick was also found in the rearview mirror of the rental car. Their solution, of course, is to interview the wife, give her a glass of water, and trick her into giving them her lip print in this manner.

Horatio then corners Cole and asks who has keys to his apartment. Cole points out that Wendy's ex doesn't have keys, but that they've come home and somehow found him in their apartment. Cut to an interview with the ex, who says that he was only in the apartment to make sure that Cole didn't have any guns or porn.

Horatio puts his thinking cap on and remembers that the plant in the hotel room was wilted. He examines the electricity usage records for the hotel room and comes to the conclusion that someone cranked the air conditioning for awhile to lower the vic's body temperature and confuse the coroner as to time of death. This clears Cole but not Michael.

The lip prints, of course, match the lipstick left on the glove so they conclude that Malcom was a hired killer, and that Greta hired him. But how could she come to Miami and then in one day, meet an assassin and hire him? Answer: Malcom's older brother lived in Germany. Greta offered him money to kill her husband, and he in turn got his little brother to do the deed.

Horatio realizes that since Cole's wife didn't know about the stabbing incident in college, someone else must have. Someone else who had access to Cole's apartment. He realizes that landlords run background checks on tenants and decide to pay Cole's landlords a visit. The missus opens the door and Horatio and the detective chat with her and notice, first of all, the forensics books lining the shelves of the house. Horatio excuses himself to use the restroom and finds cardamom soap on the sink ledge. He proceeds to take a sample, and then asks Mrs. Bastille for information about the soap.

Turns out—his idea of intimacy is to make his wife lie really still in the bathtub while he bathes her. Horatio breaks it to her that a hooker is dead and was bathed in cardamom soap so if she could tell him where her husband was on Wednesday night, it would be a big help. She says that he claimed to get a call from a tenant and took off. She is pretty upset about her husband being with and possibly killing a hooker and all so she's a little edgy. Horatio says "I want to search your apartment, but first, I want to get you out of here for your personal safety. Can I do that?"

She hustles out and he goes to town—sampling mold from the bathroom to match to the bedcover from the hotel, and finding a print in plumber's putty. The print, as it turns out, is Cole's.

Of course, Mr. Bastille is dragged into the tank and cops to the crime in about forty five seconds and Horatio takes the wrongfully arrested man back to his house and his family.

Bunk

A couple chases a cat into a seemingly abandoned house. The husband drops dead from the noxious fumes and the wife passes out.

Horatio et al arrive on the scene and determine that the house hosted a clandestine drug lab. Deciding that the services of the hazmat team are unneeded, Horatio and Speedle enter the house and determine that the substance in question is nitro glycerine. They then decide that everyone else in the ten block area needs to be evacuated while they collect evidence.

Delko and Calleigh arrive at an assistant living community. The deceased is one Betty Rosen, age 81, that appears to have been beaten to death at around 2 am. Calleigh and Delko manage to find broken glass outside her window, and a piece of paper soaked in blood.

Back at Plot A, Horatio and Speedle find a plastic glove, bag it, and go to talk to the landlord of the house. The landlord is one James Wilmont, dermatologist, who explains that the house has been vacant for six months cause the last tenants bailed. Horatio threatens to arrest him for negligible homicide due to activities that were taking place in a house that he presumed to be abandoned;

Wilmont flippantly says he'll bring his lawyer the next time they meet. They go back to CSI central and examine the chemicals more carefully. They conclude that whoever whipped up the concoction in the house was either trying to make X and failed; or purposefully trying to make something he could sell as X and accidentally made something fatal.

Back on the Betty tip: poor old Betty has Alzheimer's and appeared to have sustained injuries from trying to fight off her attacker. They do find evidence that she had sexual contact, but there was no sperm in the semen, meaning the perp had a vasectomy.

And elsewhere, Speedle finds a print on the latex glove collected from the abandoned house, and matches it to one Gregory Kimble. Kimble, as it turns out, has chemical burns on parts of his face, doesn't seem very bright, is a part time student, and drives a fancy Lexus. He is immediately booked and processed.

Things are looking worse and worse for Betty's retirement community: not only did they leave her alone even though she had Alzheimer's, the window washer is a convicted rapist. Keith Sewell, the rapist, is brought in for questioning but since he has not been snipped, they swab him and let him go.

Kimble is in luck because his lawyer actually knows the law, unlike other lawyers that Horatio has faced down. Anyway, the lawyer points out that the print on the glove only puts him at a party house; it doesn't make him a drug manufacturer. The chemicals on his shirt do match some on the scene, but they are not illegal, so he's broken no laws at this point. Horatio is forced to let him go. The next morning, however, Horatio learns that the dermatologist owns several houses in bad neighborhoods, and decides to pay them a visit. He, Speedle, and Sevilla cruise down to another one of the properties and find Kimble loading non-illegal chemicals into the place. Wilson provides the house and the chemicals, it turns out, and gets a piece of the action. They aren't selling anything illegal, but can turn a profit.

At the retirement home, Calleigh and Delko learn that Betty may have had consensual sex on the night of the attack since she had no shortage of suitors. They interview the suitors, one of whom suggests that Betty's sister Pearl—who was out with friends on the evening of the murder—offed her for her money. They also interview an ex named Mr. Gaines who has a piece of plant in his shoe that matches the plants outside Betty's window.

And on the A train, a 19 year old kid dies from what is presumed to be an X overdose. Apparently he took one, and when he didn't get high, he took a lot more and dropped dead. Anyway Alexx manages to extract the pills from his stomach; they have a diamond sun stamp on them. Wilson said he and his real estate partners had a company called Diamond Sun.

After interviewing hordes of suitors and learning that their alibis checked out, Calleigh and Delko finally decide to get around to reading the piece of paper that was submerged in the pool of blood. It says:

"It was great that you called on Friday. I was just back from my trip to Hawaii and I stopped by the office to pick up any upcoming work. I was able to draft the amendment to your will over the weekend. I'm sure you would be happy to know that all things will be in good hands. We have made the changes you asked for and it is a done deal. Don't worry about this amendment any further. The amendment will read as follows: This is to inform you the Codicil to your will has been completed and signed and is effective as of Nov. 04 2002. I hope this will put a smile on your face as we put this will to rest."

And of course, on the A plot, Greg Kimble is dead and can't be arrested. He is in a car, and appears to have been killed range. Speedle takes out a device that maps heat or something, and figures that the person in the car next to him braced himself while doing the deed. There's a big blank spot on the seat though, where they don't see any heat on the fancy doodad, and decide to go to the lab to figure it out. It turns out to be bandages from a recent carcinoma removal. Or so Horatio surmises anyway. They call Wilson into the tank and yep, he has bandages that match the pattern of heat left on the seat. And what do you know? He carries a knife for protection, and it has Kimble's blood on it.

As for Betty, Calleigh and Delko look at the blood pattern in the apartment. They determine that she fell and hit her head, and then wandered around bleeding on everything and stumbling and banging herself up on all the other hard surfaces in her apartment and died. The fact that she'd changed the will to leave everything to Pearl was a coincidence.

The end.

Forced Entry

A man in a swank pad skinny dips in his pool, and gets dressed while listening to the radio. He is interrupted by a knock at the door, and, appearing to know the person knocking, opens it.

Cut to Horatio and some nameless detective surveying the property, summoned by Girl Scouts who saw blood and an open door and called 911. The swimmer is now dead, spread eagled on the bed, his hands taped together. There is no sign of forced entry, and no valuables appear to have been tampered with, so robbery is ruled out as a motive. There appears to be some confusion as to who this guy is, though, since the Porsche in the driveway is registered to a Richard Lee Hauschild, and the house is listed under Deveraux Jones, and his watch is engraved to a Mr. Zach Kelsey. When brought back to the morgue, we learn that he was "violently sodomized" with a rusty pipe, and that he died of suffocation when fabric stuffed in his mouth was sucked down his throat. Horatio finds a tattoo and wonders if that would be a good way to ID the man. The tattoo is of a pistol, and they soon find an identical tattoo in the database beloning to one Danny Blue.

Calleigh and Delko enter a crematorium that appears to have been stashed with bodies, perhaps so the proprietor could extract gold fillings, or sell their organs. There seem to be 27 bodies piled in the back, and one half-baked in the crematorium. The motive remains unclear. The proprietor, Benito Ramon, is clutching a VIP pass to a resort/club called Canvas, and appears to have been beaten to death. One of the bodies, a young lady last seen in evening wear, had been reported missing.

Back at CSI, Danny Blue is called in for questioning, accompanied by his parole officer. We learn that the dead man is Thomas Carpenter, and that he did robberies with Danny, but only ol' Danny boy was pinched. They ask him for a hair sample, which he is obliged to give without a warrant since he is a convicted felon on parole. As it turns out, he was in Carpenter's place a couple days ago, but got in a fight with him and subsequently was kicked out. Carpenter owed him money for not having ratted him out; Carpenter, however, saw things differently. They return to the scene of the crime to see if there is any evidence they may have looked over. Horatio finds a square of paisley pattered fabric, and bags it. Speedle finds an expensive diamond necklace reported missing by one Judy Johnson. Mr. Carpenter, as it turned out, relieved Ms. Johnson of her necklace and then tied her to the bed and sodomized her. The fact that he was assaulted in the same manner that she was makes her a suspect. Or rather, would have made her a suspect if she hadn't offed herself a week after the rape.

Horatio and Delko then invite themselves to the home of Mr. Johnson, who at first is hoping that they found the rapist and have come to give him the good news. Mr. Johnson's mood quickly turns, however, when he realizes that the police are there to help the man who raped his wife. In his typically insensitive manner, Horatio asks him for the scissors that his wife used in her suicide attempt to see if they could have been used to cut the tape that bound Tom Carpenter.

They return to CSI and do more research, discovering that three other women have been Carpenter's victims, and all were sodomized after being liberated of valuable possessions.

Back at plot B, Calleigh and Delko have arrived at Canvas with a warrant, and the proprietors of said club immediately lawyer up. Calliegh and Delko survey the place and note that drops of the fluorescent paint on the walls were found on the body of the young woman in evening wear that had been reported missing—Michelle Carter. They obtain a list of VIP types, and of employees, and learn that Benito was indeed a VIP member and Michelle was a go-go dancer at the club.

Later at the morgue, Alexx points out a bruise on Michelle's face that only became visible under a UV light: it is in the shape of a C. The proprietors were wearing tacky C–shaped diamond rings that match the shape of the bruise. Calleigh calls in the proprietors and breaks the news to them that they have to surrender their ugly rings. The rings have no epithelials or crematorium ash on them, so at first this seems like a waste of time, but then Guerro becomes angry, and lets it slip that Michelle was go-go dancing for them with the understanding that she was not to work anywhere else. Michelle nonetheless decided to promote for a club called the Thorny Rose, and "stepped on toes in the process."

Elsewhere, Speedle looks over the evidence taken from Carpenter's house in hopes of finding a clue. He has variety of stolen valuables engraved with the names of the rightful owners, and the piece of fabric that choked the victim. He takes the fabric to the lab for analysis and learns that it is carried at ten stores in the Miami area. One such store is owned by a couple—Leonard and Erin Murphy-- who seem to have been liberated of a valuable, engraved crystal vase found in Carpenter's home.

Speedle pays Leonard and Erin Murphy's home décor store a visit and learns that they never reported their vase missing. At first, not realizing he's with Miami Dade PD, Erin asks him if he'd like to be on the mailing list. Speedle looks at the clipboard and sees Thomas Carpenter's name all over it. Speedle chews on this, and then notes the rusty pipes along the wall, and watches Erin cut some ribbon with a pair of scissors. He then asks Erin for a sample of her hair, and all the scissors in the place, and then drags her into the tank for questioning.

The interrogation opens with Erin incredulously saying: "You think I was raped? I think you've got some wrong information. I can assure you, if I was raped, trust me, the police would know about it." Horatio asks "Why didn't you report your home being burglarized?" "Because it wasn't!" Erin protests. Horatio shows her photo of the anniversary vase and asks, "Do you own one of these?" Erin says that she did, but it shattered into a million pieces. She says "It fell off the shelf while my husband was moving furniture. He called me while I was overseas buying fabric to tell me." Horatio says acidly, "Your trips. Your fabric-buying trips." Erin, still confused, says "Yes, fabric-buying trips. I spent two weeks in India. I just got back last night."

On the Plot B tip, Calleigh learns that there were more than two of those tacky C rings made. They search the residences of all owners and find one at the home of the club's legal counsel, Mr. Graziano. Calleigh takes Graziano in for questioning and gets him to admit that Michelle was soliciting the VIP clients of his club to come watch her dance at other clubs. So Graziano strangled Michelle after punching her and getting some of her epithelials in his ugly ring. Then he took her to ol' Benito's crematorium and asked him to dispose of the body and her belongings in return for a VIP pass. Upon returning to check Benito's work, however, he saw that Benito had not followed instructions. He then got some of his epithelials on his ring as well when he beat and killed Benito.

They drag Leonard in for questioning and learn that it was not his wife, but him that was bound, robbed, and sodomized. Carpenter came into his store one day and didn't recognize him. Leonard got him to write down his mailing address, and went to the house after work one day and killed him.

Dead Woman Walking

Horatio is summoned to check out the body of a man found dead at the foot of a stairwell, an enormous syringe next to him but no signs of an OD. The man, as it turns out, is named Carl Aspen, and has a long rap sheet of petty crimes.

Alexx arrives to examine him, and determines that he died between 4 and 6 am. His nails are torn, so she bags his hands in hopes of finding DNA, and when she turns him over, she notes $203 in cash in his pockets and a chewed up pencil. Back at the morgue, she determines the cause of death: his neck was broken. She pulls his hands out of the bag but the skin has deteriorated. Puzzled, she shows Horatio and he immediately leads her away from the body and tells her that the man seems to have radiation poisoning. He hits the panic button and the building is evacuated.

When the coast is clear and the building has been neutralized, Horatio puzzles over how this man could have such acute radiation poisoning. He wonders if the contents of the giant syringe had anything to do with it. Did he mug someone who was self-administering radiation therapy, perhaps, and inject himself since he mistook it for smack? Maybe a terrorist planning to do something insidious with a syringe full of radioactive isotopes who then snapped Carl's neck and ran away without the syringe?

Horatio examines the chewed up pencil and sees that it is stamped with the name of a lawyer: Belle King, attorney at law, environmental law specialist. They go over there with a warrant and a Geiger counter. When they get to her place, the radiation detector goes crazy and they get her out of the office and to a hospital. There we learn that she is not contagious, but has one week to live.

Understandably, she's a bit shaken, so she and Horatio go for a hot dog and discuss possible enemies that would want her dead. She comes up with a list of companies that she is suing, all of whom have to do with nuclear radiation and isotopes etc, but none served her anything to eat or drink.

Speedle goes to her office, and gets her assistant to open the locked file cabinet. Inside is a candy box filled with several rolls of film and a camera. At her house, Calleigh has concluded that nothing has been tainted with the poison she was given, and Horatio notices a basket of flowers that had been sent anonymously. They also find an angry letter from a man named Sam Carver that reads:

"Dear Belle

Or should I call you Jezebelle for the way you have betrayed us. Janet is so upset about Michael she's holed up in bed and can hardly get up. She's crying non-stop. You made promises and gave us hope but then you couldn't deliver. I don't want to see the same thing happen with Hank. That's why I writing to tell you to stay the hell away from us. Every time you leave a message its like a bullet in our hearts. You may not keep your promises but I do and I promise that if you don't let this thing with hank go there will be a bullet for you. If you ever try to contact us again I'll kill you and that's a promise."

Belle explains, "He wrote that right after his oldest son died. It was horrible. I still wanted to fight for Hank. He's seven now, he's doing fine, we worked everything out. In fact, Janet [his wife] still leaves me fresh orange juice every couple of days to celebrate the clean new water." Uh oh. Did she drink the orange juice? She sure did! Calleigh tests the remains and it is indeed the source of the poison she took.

Horatio interviews the Carvers and examines the container that the orange juice was delivered in. He concludes that the culprit is not Mr. Carver; the culprit knew that the orange juice had been left for Belle, and injected it after the fact.

Meanwhile, Delko has been examining the $203 found on Aspen, and has realized that there is a credit card imprint on one of the bills. The imprint belongs to a George Risher, of Risher pharmaceuticals, who, incidentally, stands to lose $128 million if Ms. King wins the lawsuit she brought against him.

Horatio and a detective then hotfoot it to Risher Pharm, which is three blocks away from where Aspen was found dead. Horatio also notes that there are radioactive isotopes are roughly twenty feet from the door, and that there's a new lock on the facility. Meanwhile, Delko and Calleigh poke around the building and immediately discover that radioactive isotopes are kept next to people's sack lunches in the lab fridge. Calleigh also finds a muddy boot-print on the floor near the fridge.

At CSI central, Speedle has been developing the photos that he found in the candy box. He shows the results to the others: the photos are of the Risher lab, only taken at night. They realize that they put Belle inside the lab, and wonder if she left the boot print that was on the floor.

Horatio asks Belle about it, and she says that the photos were taken by an inside source that she can't reveal. Delko then examines the camera in an effort to figure out the source, and realizes that whoever took the pictures was farsighted. They narrow down 14 Risher employees that are farsighted, and then swab them in an effort to match DNA with the epithelials found under Carl's fingernails.

The DNA all points to the secretary, Boyd, who is immediately arrested and brought into the tank. As it turns out, he was mugged by Carl, after poisoning Belle, and in the scuffle that ensued, he snapped Carle's neck. Why? Because he loved her and she didn't love him back, he says.

Horatio breaks the news to Belle, and tells her that he will still help move the case forward. She whispers a thank you, and the screen goes dark.

Evidence of Things Unseen

A man patronizing a peep show is stabbed to death in a booth. Anyway, the dancer in the booth saw nothing because he was stabbed when the gate snapped shut because he ran out of quarters. Horatio and Alexx quickly realize he was stabbed through the door with an eight inch serrated blade. There was a peephole in the door to the booth so the perp would know when and where to aim.

At the morgue, they learn that he was stabbed twice, and that each stab wound is in a t-shape. Calleigh examines the wounds and theorizes that they were made by either Gryphon M35, a recon with a tanto point, or an Echelon MPT.

That settled, Horatio returns to the peep show to talk to the dancer that was working the booth when the guy was stabbed. She didn't see anything, however, so Horatio lets her leave without dragging her into the tank.

Delko, meanwhile, is puzzling over a hair taken from the floor of the crime scene. It seems to be, of all things, an ape hair. So they head to the Miami Zoo. After flashing pictures to the monkey house guys, the deceased is ID'd as Victor Ratsch, custodian. His cousin Vadim got him the job. Oh and they were always fighting.

Horatio is torn away from the zoo when his cell rings and we learn that the stripper from a couple scenes ago was killed in a hit and run. Alexx digs some paint chips and glass out of the victim's leg, and Horatio pays a visit to her now-widowed husband, Rick Breck. Rick doesn't seem too broken up about his wife's death. She walked home from work at 2 am as usual cause they didn't have a car. She left a message before she came home but since it wasn't out of the ordinary, he erased it. So Horatio takes the machine with him.

As they leave, Horatio thinks that getting a warrant would be a good idea because they don't have probably cause. The nameless cop with him, says "The probable cause is she's a stripper, she's a junkie, and she's a whore." "She's also a human being," Horatio says, and the cop says "She's also a corpse, and by God, don't you ever step on my investigation again."

At the lab, Delko has pieced together the message Amy left before she died: "Hey, Rick, I'm on the way. Did you get stuff you promised you'd pick up? After tonight, I could really use some. Ace, hi. Don't start without me, okay?" After dialing down the background noise, we also hear a male voice on the tape saying "hey" and, "We got a deal."

They go to talk to Mr. Breck again but have some trouble, as he's floating face down in the marina.

They decide to talk to Vadim before he too drops dead. Delko goes with Horatio since he speaks Russian (he's Russian and Cuban remember?) and they corner Vadim at work. "Tell him that I can see by the scratches on his face that he's been in a recent altercation," Horatio says to Delko. Vadim says that a lion or a did it. "Now tell him that if I check under his fingernails, and if I can match it to his dead cousin, I'm going to arrest him for murder," Horatio says, forgetting, I guess, that the victim was stabbed through a door so skin from under the cousin's nails will get him nothing. Vadim then speaks English and says "I haven't seen my cousin in two days...Victor never goes to peep show," says Vadim, and he doesn't either: "I don't have to pay money for women. At peepshow? Lap dance, you spend $5. Another $5. $20 here. $20 there. By end of night, you could have banged a hooker." Yakov points at Horatio. "He knows what I'm talking about."

Then the truth comes out vis-à-vis the scratches: Two nights ago, Victor refused to feed the lions. So Vadim says to him, "'The lions, they scare me. I'll do anything else'. But no, that night he has to go. So I just lost it." Horatio wants to know where Victor had to be. "He only says to me, 'Is business,' Yakov says bitterly. "Big business, big man. All he has to do is look mean, which for Victor is not that difficult. He says I feed the lions, he cut me in. But I know my cousin. He give me $5, he's making $500. Plus, it's probably not legal." Horatio wants to know who Victor was supposed to scare. Vadim doesn't know.

Soon thereafter, Horatio learns that Breck's lungs were filled with toilet water. So they take a sample of the toilet water on his boat, and find an ape hair while in the process. They also find a fancy digital camera with pictures of Amy and her husband in flagrante delecto, and print it to see who snapped the pics. And Delko finds a knife behind a panel on the boat. "That's an Echelon MPT," Calleigh says. "I've only seen those at gun shows."

It's printed and Rick's prints are on it. So we know now who murdered the Russian zookeeper. And there were many, many people's semen in the bedroom too, so we know that Amy was popular with the gents. As for Amy— there were traces of elephant feces on the headlight that was embedded in her leg when she was run over.

The car is identified as one owned by one Mr. Infante, reported stolen two days ago. Infante is also a regular at the peep show who always requested Amy. Funny enough, his ejaculate was found at the foot of Amy and Rick's bed. In comes Infante for questioning.

"You can't possibly be here because I watched two people having sex within the privacy of their own bedroom," Infante says. No. He's here so Horatio can accuse him of murder based on circumstantial evidence. Infante admits that Breck and his wife were blackmailing him, but he says he paid up and scoffs at Horatio's attempts to pin murder on him.

Tests from the car come back and of course, they find Infante's prints on it. But they also find the prints of Mr. Davis, the owner of the peep show, and place him behind the wheel of the car. He finally cops to all of it: he murdered Amy and her husband for not cutting him in on the blackmail take.

In the next scene, Horatio goes to the peep show. He drops a couple of hundreds into the booth's slot. "Well, what do you want for this?" she. "I want you to take the rest of the day off," he says. "What about tomorrow?" the stripper asks. "Tomorrow is what you make of it," Horatio says.

Simple Man

The show opens with a media circus surrounding one Councilwoman Escalante, braving the media fray because her husband is on trial for murdering their housekeeper, Abby Sandoval, after having an affair with her.

Horatio is pulled away from the courtroom just before he is about to testify because he's informed that a young woman is in the morgue, and her death may have some bearing on the Escalante case. He rushes to the morgue and Alexx gives him a rundown: "Like looking in a mirror. Both victims in their early twenties, pretty, Latina, shot once in the head, left temple, mint leaves in the stomach, both worked with their hands. Now, I'm thinking Jane Doe might have been a domestic just like Abby was." Horatio finds this problematic. She couldn't have been killed by Lorenzo Escalante because he was in custody at the time of her death. How were they different?" Well, not very. Abby was shot in her car, this one was found dumped on the roadside.

Horatio orders Calleigh to compare the bullet found in Jane Doe to the one found in Abigail Sandoval, and asks Delko to see if any fibers were found on Juana Doe that match fibers found on Abigal.

The DA learns of this shortly, however, and is not pleased. He confronts Horatio and says: "Lorenzo Escalante. He had an affair with the maid. He admits to getting rough with her. He got his semen inside of her, his DNA under her fingernails." Horatio counters that they don't have the gun. Don the DA doesn't particularly care; that's what appeals are for, he says, and stalks off.

Horatio joins Sevilla and Delko at the road where Juana Doe was found. He surmises that she was not killed where she was found; he says, "She crawled to here. Probably rested for a moment, losing a lot of blood. Continued to travel, and then somehow got up. Fell again right here." They walk along the road and notice a car submerged in the adjunct canal. "So [Jane Doe] crawled from here all the way to the road." Delko adds, "A quarter of a mile on her belly with a 9-mm round in her head. All for nothing." "Not if we can help it," Horatio says.

They drag the car out of the canal and find check-cashing card belonging to one Bonita Cruz of Southwest 10th Street. Delko comments "I know a lot of girls like that. They come from Cuba, Honduras, Nicaragua, looking for a better life, but they wind up cleaning toilets in Bal Harbour." Delko finds a shell casing.

Calleigh, meanwhile, has been assigned to help one Detective Hagen with the ballistics involved in a highway shooting, and has put that aside to help Horatio with the bullet comparison situation. Hagen is unthrilled: "I'm sorry . Am I bothering you here in your nice, air-conditioned crime lab? 'Cause I'm sweating my butt off trying to get my causeway shooter into arraignment." She assures him that it will get done but she needs more time.

Back on the Bonita Cruz tip, Delko has matched fibers from her to ones taken from Abigail. They both come from $2,000 suits. He has also found a snippet of a Cuban-American newspaper that says:

EMPLEOS DOMESTICOS
Externa 5 dias. Refen
6300. sem.
305-555-0179

Could the murderer have found these women with this ad? They drag the canal once again to find the gun or any other evidence. They find the gun, and a circled newspaper ad offering $600 a week for domestic work.

They hunt down the person who traced the ad and though they are unable to pin down a specific person, as the ad was placed via mail, they know it was placed by someone in Councilwoman Mercedes Escalante's office complex.

Escalante is as helpful as ever, offering a list of everyone who has worked in the office in the past year, and producing it on the spot—it's written on a notepad and they take the whole pad. Horatio is somewhat suspicious and pulls Sevilla aside. Sevilla confirms that she told Mercedes that they were coming—it was a courtesy heads-up since they grew up together. Horatio is displeased. Horatio does not like this. His mood is buoyed considerably, however, when Calleigh matches the bullet used to kill Cruz with the one that killed Sandoval.

Horatio runs to the courtroom and saves the day. As the judge lets Mr. Escalante go, the camera lingers on the missus giving a sheepish look.

Back at the lab, the CSIs wearily look at news footage of Mr. Escalante as a free man. Delko contends that there were two murders; Speedle asks him to explain the same gun, the same fibers, and the same type of mint leaf involved in both. Horatio walks in and says " Maybe he did have the details [to the first murder], and that would make him a copycat, wouldn't it?"

Horatio explains it thusly: the killer just had to advertise for a housekeeper in a Spanish-only newspaper, using a disposable cell phone. Once she's hired, the killer followed her in his (or her) vehicle, pulled her over, and shot her with the gun from the first murder, then planted fibers and pushed the car in the canal.

First, to the morgue! Here, Alexx explains how the wound track in Bonita's head does not line up with the hole shot through the driver's side window. Why? There were two shots. And why was that? The killer didn't count on Bonita rolling down her window.

Enter Carmen Abregon, as procured by Sevilla. She's one of the forty-three women tracked down via cell phone records. She responded to the ad in El Diario. Carmen, in Spanish, says she met the man who placed the ad off Hwy 41, but got a bad feeling. For one, he was wearing gloves. In the summer. And for two, he ordered her a mojito as a "yay you're hired!" kind of gesture. She is asked to work with the police artist, and they come up with a sketch that looks just like Carlos Galaz, Escalante's handler.

He is brought in for questioning and doesn't take it too well. "You know what you just did? Your career is over. When I'm through with you, you're going to be doing timecards at county lockup." Horatio notes, "Still got the phone, Carl. You've still got the phone." Once they pull it out of the briefcase, Sevilla says, "You've still got seven dollars of call time left, Carl. Seven dollars in exchange for the rest of your life." The scene ends with Galaz being taken to central booking while Horatio stares at a giant Mercedes Escalante poster.

Galaz returns some time later, having lawyered up, to face Horatio in the interrogation tank. Horatio opens with "Carl, I think I understand what's going on here. You killed Bonita Cruz to get Lorenzo off the hook for murder -- I understand that part. What I'm curious about is whose gun was it?" Carl says it's his gun and then the lawyer whistles a little tune called "I've advised my client to say nothing more." Carl doesn't like this tune and insists that he killed both women.

Horatio then pays a visit to Speedle, who has been analyzing the notepad that the councilwoman gave them when she procured the list of all office employees. He says "I measured stroke depth and I isolated the layers. There are seven pages, each dating back week-by-week. We get to the fifth week, he writes a to-do list -- buy gloves, clean gun, disposable cell phone." In the second week, however, there is a completely different handwriting sample that says : "BBQ 7A 3D," and continues, "Barbecue. That's not a lunch order⋯guess whose handwriting that is? I got this [other sample] from public records -- a city lease drafted by Lorenzo Escalante."

Horatio heads over to the Escalante's house with Sevilla. They search the yard and find nothing. Then they search the barbeque, and sure enough, there's a lockbox containing Golden Talon bullets like the ones they took out of Abby Sandoval and Benita Cruz. They hightail it to the country club and re-arrest him while he plays golf.

He then accuses the councilwoman of intending to pardon her husband once she's in the governer's mansion; she responds icily that he should watch his step.

The episode ends with Horatio asking a colleague, Elena, to go out, and they leave for coffee.

CSI Miami: Season One

Dispo Day

Horatio et al are riding in the CSI mobile to dispose of evidence wherever it is that one disposes of evidence. Flashbacks indicate that the evidence in question is a lot of cocaine. As they blithely roll along, a funeral procession with a police escort makes its way towards the CSI motorcade. Horatio advises the driver of his humvee to let the funeral procession pass. But the patrolman with the funeral possession looks somewhat suspicious, and is positioned in the three way stop so no one can pass. As Horatio's spidey senses start tingling, a station wagon plows into the hearse. Now no one can pass.

The faux cop throws a smoke bomb type thing into the fray and two people get out of the hearse brandishing semi-automatics. Meanwhile, the woman in the station wagon is hysterically trying to get her baby out of the baby seat.

Horatio bounds out of his vehicle to save the woman, and as he does, Speedle tries to fire at a bad guy but his gun jams. The bad guy instead shoots him in the chest, and takes command of Horatio's vehicle (the one with the drugs in it) while Horatio tells the hysterical woman to stay down. He turns as the vehicle drives off, and manages to shoot out one of the tires.

Horatio then realizes that Speedle has been shot in the chest and runs to him. He has Kevlar on, which caught the bullet, but has had the wind knocked out of him and writhes on the ground for a bit. EMTs appear—the mother was shot in the arm, but will be ok. The baby's unharmed. A couple of the guys who were escorting them in the disposal motorcade didn't make it.

They eventually get around to inspecting the crime scene and note immediately that the hearse was stolen, as evidenced by the screwdriver in the ignition. Calleigh digs an enormous bullet out of the upholstery and explains that these types of slugs have been off the market since 1997.

As Horatio arrives at CSI central, the reporters are already converging. One with particularly offensive hair accosts him and after introducing himself to Horatio and the people at home says: "Just drawing a parallel here. Your brother gave his life in the line of duty two years ago, albeit under much cloudier circumstances --" "Circumstances weren't cloudy -- the reporting was," Horatio snarks. He is interrupted when he receives word that the truck was found.

Curiously, millions of dollars of heroin and speed were left untouched but the cocaine is gone. Everyone decides that the flat tire limited the amount of drugs that could be transported away, everyone took only what they could carry. They also find the discarded police uniform, and blood.

Horatio's day gets worse when he's confronted by a SWAT guy on the way back to CSI. Thinking that someone leaked the dispo route, the swat guy says he'll be needed everyone on Horatio's team to take a lie detector test.

The uniforms were stolen from a dry cleaner ten days ago, which was the same time they decided to dispose of the drugs.

Delko is first to take the test. It opens with "were you born in Miami?" and the next question is "what's four time six plus three?" because mental calculations show up as lies. The next question is "Have you ever lied to someone who loved and trusted you?" xWhile Delko is sitting through the polygraph, Horatio checks out the station wagon. He notes that the station wagon is spotless and remembers that the woman was screaming THE baby. Not MY baby.

Horatio pays Lynn (the woman) a visit. He asks her what day her son was born. She says she thinks it was a Friday. Horatio says, "If we can prove that you were paid to hit that car, we can charge you with Murder One." Lynn tells him: "I didn't know that there was going to be the shooting.

I got paid $5000 to wait for the funeral procession, then slam into the hearse." Horatio asks who paid her. She says, "Somebody else contacted him, and he presses further: "But somebody was shooting at you. We have the forensics to prove it. Trajectory says it was intentional. So why don't you give me a name?" She immediately says, "Dr. Guillermo Santoya."

Cut to Horatio digging around the offices of Dr. Guillermo Santoya. He looks in a trash can and sees bloody gauze and a bullet and asks who the bullet came out of. He says: Cassidy. This Cassidy person was brought in this morning. Santoya advised him to go to a hospital; his buddies declined and dropped him at the Hialeah.

The next scene is of the swat team converging on a darkened room where Cassidy is bleeding. Horatio squeezes Cassidy's wound and asks for a name. Cassidy says: Nedir Kire and then dies.

Calleigh, meanwhile, has found 122 pieces of firearm evidence. "So the round count on our two officers is fifty-four. Out of that, I got forty-five casings. Those are shown in blue." There are also twelve bullets. She continues "It was the usual yield -- three-fourths of the casings, one-fourth of the bullets." Horatio says, "The ex-cons used Tec-9s, didn't they?" Calleigh says yes, and tells him she got forty casings and eighteen bullets, one of which killed Hollis. Not only that, the bullet from Lynn's car came from across the street, so someone was aiming to take her out too.

The next scene is of Speedle's polygraph test, which is a lot more fun to watch than Delko's was, so I'll give you the blow by blow:

Tech: "Did you come here intending to lie?"
Speedle: "No."
Tech: "Did you take part in an officer-involved shooting yesterday?"
Speedle: "Your phraseology is misleading."
Tech: "Please answer 'yes' or 'no.'"
Speedle: "Please rephrase the question."
Tech: "If you fail to cooperate..."
Speedle: "Was I involved in a shootout? Yeah. Was an officer killed? Yes."
Tech asks: "Did you disclose any information regarding the narcotics transport?"
Speedle: "No"
Tech: "The officer riding next to you was shot in the head. Was his name Officer Hollis?"
Speedle: "yes".
Tech: "Did your vest protect you from serious injury?"
Speedle: "yes". [but oddly, here his reading spikes].

Tech: "Did the suspects have any reason to kill Officer Hollis but only wound you?"
Speedel: "This game is over. I'm sorry, but I have an officer-involved shooting to investigate, so no time for this petty crap." [here the readings spike and he takes off.]

As he leaves, Calleigh sees him in the hall and trots after him. He blows up at her: peedle bursts out, "My gun misfired, okay? I admit it. It misfired because I didn't clean it. That's why it jammed up, and that's why Hollis is dead. Okay? And I should probably resign." Calleigh says "That is not true. That was an ambush. He was shot from the left-hand side and there's nothing that you could have done about it...Just next time it could be you...clean your gun."

She then proceeds to some kind of alleyway She's in an alleyway dotted with bullet holes. Detective Frank pulls up in his car and says, "This place looks like a battle zone. Look at all the stray gunfire." Calleigh says, "I'm not as concerned about the ones going in as the one that came out...I think this gives us cause to search the place." They knock on the door and a fabio wannabe answers. She says: "Do you always work on Sundays?" The croons "Only when I am expecting a visit from an angel." Calleigh asks if he saw anything. He tells her, "I was hiding behind the limestone. It sounded like Liberty City on the Fourth of July." Frank asks, "Do you own a firearm, Mr. Tomassi?"

He says no. Then Calleigh says that she wants to take a look around because, "It's important to recover all of the rounds in an officer-involved shooting."

She ends up by a bunch of dusty limestone, and pulls out a shell.

Cut to Calleigh's polygraph, where she answers negatively to the question: "did you take any drugs or alcohol in an attempt to influence this exam". The tech says, "Did you process evidence for dispo day?" Calleigh did. The tech asks, "Was that drug cocaine?" It sure was! Calleigh is given a cup to pee in.

In the next scene, Jack informs Horatio that she will have to be suspended because she tested positive for cocaine. Horatio drags Calleigh aside and she swears up and down she's never taken drugs. He asks her how she feels, and where she has been. Answer to question one: confused, angry, confused. Question two: Tripp and I were trying to follow the mystery trajectory. We went to the tile place. I ate a granola bar. Uh, then we went back to the firearms lab. She says she found a bullet lodged in marble tile and had to struggle to dig it out.

Horatio tests the bullet; it has cocaine on it.

Tomassi is dragged in and after watching Horatio destroy sheets of his marble, confesses. The cocaine is suspended in a plaster-like organic adhesive which lets the cocaine harden, and when it's time to move the drug, they simply wash the paste solid. Tomassi does not, however, cop to getting his cocaine from the crime scene. Horatio again proves him wrong by putting the cocaine through some kind of process that allows him to separate bits of crime scene tape from it.

Deko, meanwhile, has nothing on Nedir Kire. Until he realizes that it's Erik Riden backwards. He plugs the name into google can comes up with Enrique Rayas, the reporter who accosted Horatio when he first got back from the doomed dispo.

So the way it went down: the incinerator operator told Rayas, and Rayas participated so he could boost his ratings as a reporter

Basically Horatio tells Speedle to clean his gun more often and that's that.

CSI Miami: Season One

Double Cap

The thin, tan, and beautiful lounge by a pool somewhere in Miami. As the afternoon sun turns golden, a cabana boy notes a woman who is severely sunburned. He tries to wake her, and failing, removes the hat that is covering her face. He drops it like a hot potato and scurries off, grimacing.

Horatio, crime fighting mastermind, arrives on the scene and deduces from the bullet hole in her head that she was shot.

A perimeter search fails to lead to a bullet or a casing. Alexx takes a close look at the victim and notices that there is searing around the wound, meaning she had the gun to her head, and Horatio learns from the guy at the front desk that her name is Gloria Tynan. Gloria, as it turns out, checks into the penthouse every Tuesday afternoon with an unnamed man, and pays cash. Horatio thinks that given that she paid cash, it's odd that she only has $10 in her $300 purse.

Cut to Speedle and Delko in an elevator that for some reason a tv screen in it showing footage of the pool. They decide that the shooter could have been captured on security camera. Anyway they are taking the elevator to Ms. Tynan's room. They give it a once-over and Delko finds a print, and Speedle finds porn. He thinks that this is mystifying since Gloria is hot.

And at the morgue, Alexx confirms that she was actually shot twice in the head, and has fished out the bullets to give to Calleigh. Horatio scans Gloria's prints, and while he waits for the computer to process them, we go to Speedle, who is viewing the security camera footage. Gloria's cabana obstructed a lot of the view, however, Speedle does note that she asked for a phone despite having a cel phone with her.

Calleigh, meanwhile, picks her drunk father up from a bar in a scene which is supposed to add depth to the character. She then returns to work and determines that the perp used a silencer. Interestingly, he bullets match those found in an unsolved four-year-old robbery case out in Uleta, and Horatio's sister in law was the detective on the case.

At the lab, the computer has processed Gloria's prints. When it comes up, Horatio realizes that for some reason, Gloria has been flagged by the feds. Because her file has been accessed, the feds will probably want to speak to them shortly.

No matter; he's off to talk to his sister in law. Elena hands him the file on the robbery, saying "Savings and loan in

Uleta. Two suspects, ski masks, .22s, terrorized the tellers and got away with 600K in cash...the teller noticed a dark mole on one suspect's neck." Horatio tells her about the murder, takes the file, and goes on his merry way.

Back at CSI central, Delko has pulled up more information: she has no priors, drives a dodge Neon, and reported a theft six months ago at her job. It "turns out Jeff Gabler's father owns the place. Runs a day tour to the Keys and back." Horatio says: "Wait a sec -- Jeff Gabler, Lieutenant Gabler from Narco?" Yep, sure is. Gloria lost her wallet and reported it stolen but "cops never found the guy." Horatio =says, "That's because there is no guy and we are being detoured into the land of make-believe." Delko asks, "Are you talking about the Feds?" Horatio explains, "When they put you under protection, for whatever reason, they make up a story based on cops and cops' families." Delko realizes, "They'll keep the story straight." Additionally, he figured out what number she called when she used the hotel phone instead of her cell phone: Coconut Grove. 2420 Lyons Ave.

Detective John and Horatio hotfoot it to the address. It's a giant stucco house with lots of lush landscaping. They show the woman who answers the door the picture of Gloria on the morgue table and asks if she knows Gloria. The woman says: "I don't know where you got that name 'Gloria.' It's

Gina. This is my daughter. I haven't seen her in over a year." Horatio says, "You knew she lived in Miami, didn't you?" The woman says, "I didn't know where." Horatio tells her, "Because she couldn't tell you. Did she have a man in her life?" She did but the mother doesn't know his name. He gave Gina/Gloria lots of expensive presents and pressured Gina's mom to wear a gigantic tacky ring. Horatio asks, "Do you have the box the ring came in?" As she looks, Hagen asks, "You move in recently, Mrs. Cusak?" Why, yes, she did. Gina had asked her to. Although Mrs. Cusak never saw Gina, they talked every Tuesday afternoon at the same time when Gina would call. Hagen asks, "On that cordless phone?" Mrs. Cusak asks, "Why? What's wrong with the phone?" "Nothing," Horatio replies.

He steps outside and immediately notices the black town car, preferred vehicle for those who baby sit people who have entered the witness protection program. Horatio knocks on the window. After the man inside rolls it down, Horatio shows him the bag the ring came in and says, "Marshall, I just got this from Gina Cusak's mom. I was going to run it for prints on the boyfriend, but after all is said and done, it would just spit out background info from your imagination, right?" "All part of protecting our witness," said the Marshall, whose name is Ardine. Horatio has already figured out what the story is on the witness:

"He's from Philly, he deals in swag -- I think I have an idea, but why don't you tell me how Gina ties into your witness." Ardine replies, "Let's just say he's a married man, and she's not his wife." Horatio says, "So you put his mistress into the program, but you didn't protect her." Ardine says, "We gave her a new life, a new identity and a new job near our primary. It's not our fault she broke protocol, contacted her mother, dragged her down from Philly." Horatio chides him for failing to monitor the phones; then Marshall tells Horatio they have a secure landline. Horatio breaks the news about the cordless and says "Gina's killer sat out here with a receiver, picked up the radio waves from the cordless, and tracked her to the Agramonte Hotel. So you guys slipped up and Gina paid. Nice going." Ardine warns Horatio off the case lest he scare the witness.

While this has happened, Delko has ID'd the print found in the hotel room. Edward Hinkle, husband to Mary and daughter to Jessica, also in the Program. He relays this to Horatio and they are interrupted by a visit from one of the Feds. Eddie, as it turns out, is preparing to testify in a federal trial against his former drug suppliers. Horatio breaks the news to him about the bank robbery, and in looking at a picture of Eddie, notices he even has the telltale mole. The Marshall insists they poly'd Eddie before putting him in the Program and that he had no priors. Horatio tells him about this, and about the murder at the pool, and uses this to get the Feds to let him meet with Mrs. Hinkle.

When he does, Mrs. Hinkle is less than pleased. "Gina? Gina from Philly? You guys brought her down here too?" Agent Sackeim says, "Her relocation was arranged also, yes." Horatio says, "can you tell us where your husband is?" she says "frank?" which causes the agent to wince and remind her that her husband's name is Eddie now. She doesn't take this well either: "Ed, Frank, Gotrocks, Mister I-Deal-In-Cash-Only, whatever, all right?" She elaborates on the cash thing, saying he has tons hidden away but she has no idea where it is; she takes what she can from his wallet. Horatio asks to see the cash she has from his wallet and she pulls out an enormous wad of hundreds, saying "Tell Frank if he hadn't kept Gina, I never would have done this.".

Back at the lab, Speedle has learned that the culprit pretended to be a towel boy, concealing the gun in a stack of towels and then offing Gloria when no one was looking. They go through the hotel laundry and find a towel with gunpowder residue, and a hair. The hair belongs to James Fukes, from PA, who has a rap sheet a mile long. Horatio concludes that James robbed the bank and Frank/Eddie got the money. By going into the program he got out of paying Jimmy, and by killing Gina, Jimmy sent a message to Frank to pay up.

They analyze the wad of cash that Mrs. Hinkle gave them and learn there are traces of Vikron, a disinfectant used on cruise ships. "So Frank asked Gina to stash his cash at work...so she's in charge of the cash. When Frank finds out she's dead --" Delko says, "He jumps on this afternoon's tour boat to grab his money. Round trip to the Keys, no stops. So if he makes it on the boat where there's no getting off, he should be back after the Regal sunset dinner."

They arrest him as he's getting off the boat, and as they take him away, a Federal Marshall appears and tells Horatio that he cannot indict his witness. Horatio agrees, if he'll deliver Fukes.

Cut to Agent Sackheim, Frank, and Horatio in a room, staring at the phone, waiting for Fukes to call so they can trace it. Finally, Fukes does call but Frank doesn't do so hot when it comes to keeping him on the line long enough to get a trace: "This is your friend from Philly," he starts. Jimmy replies "What are you, Paulie Walnuts? I know who you are, Frank. You screwed me." Frank replies, "You got my attention." Jimmy says, "You're rolling over on me, aren't you, Frank? What, do you think I'm stupid?" before hanging up.

Agent Sackheim prepares to take his witness and go, but Horatio, failing as always to see the big picture when it doesn't have him in it, refuses. Who cares if hundreds of thousands, maybe millions, of taxpayer dollars have been spent on the case that Frank is testifying in? It's about Horatio!

He presses Frank for more info, and all he gets is that Fukes likes the ponies. They promptly arrest him at the tracks.

But again, Horatio is thwarted by the Feds, who have realized that Fukes can help them build a case against the Mostello crime family, and want to absorb him into the Program.

The end.

Grave Young Men

Horatio talks to his sister in law about holiday plans and as he is heading to his car, he runs into Pete Wilton. He is a convicted felon and Horatio knows him because he put him behind bars for manslaughter and grand theft.

After Pete convinces Horatio that he's not there to kill him, Horatio relaxes a bit and Pete shows him a photograph of his son. He says that his son has been missing for three days and the cops are not interested in putting too much manpower in finding the child of a convicted felon. He butters Horatio up, telling him how good he is, how he's the best, and how he really needs his help.

In the next scene, we are introduced to plot B, the case of the naked man with bruises all over his face. The naked man was found dead by his paramour Alison when she woke up in the morning and saw him sleeping next to her in a state of partial rigor mortis, and she claims to have no idea how he died or what happened.

She flirts with Speedle but he doesn't bite, asking her why she would have such impractical nails (super long, with sparkly stars on the end of each tip), and sends her away from the crime scene.

Alexx completes her examination of the body and concludes that the victim was a distance runner, and may have suffered a cardiac situation. She says he also seems to have been asphyxiated, either by sleep apnea, or by having Miss Thing with the nails hold a pillow over his face.

Back at plot A, Horatio and Speedle rifle through Jeff's room. They find a solvent used for cleaning guns, a tee-shirt advertising his love of marijuana, and gun magazines.

Jeff also has a stash of weed and shot guns out of his bedroom window into a tree in the backyard. Delko immediately says that Pete was lying; Horatio convinces him that Pete had no idea what his son was up to—kids are sneaky. If he did, he probably wouldn't have asked two cops to search his son's room, after all.

At Plot B, Alexx discovers that the body was flipped over at some point. He died on his back, and was flipped onto his stomach. Speedle goes to talk to Miss Thing about it and asks if he can swab under her fingernails, and take pictures of the scratches on her chest.

At the CSI lab, Calleigh has cut down the tree that Jeff used for target practice, and is examining it in the lab. Delko comes in and she tells him that a lot of different kinds of ammo has been shot at the tree, and then they get into a discussion about Horatio's brother. He worked narcotics and was shot in the line of duty, leading Calleigh to infer for some reason that he was a "dirty cop."

That settled, Delko departs and Horatio enters to examine the tree. He immediately concludes that the tree wasn't for target practice, it was for some kind of training exercise. In a move that makes me think a lot less of Horatio, he turns Pete into the parole officer. The parole officer tells him that he's going to have to somehow prove that the guns, ammo, and drugs were his son's, or serve the rest of his sentence. For now, the only option available is the latter.

While Horatio is busy selling Pete down the river, Delko is breaking into Jeff's locker. He finds shoes with dirt all over it, and Gun Ho magazine.

At the lab, Calleigh has found that bullets stuck in the tree came from the gun of one Nick Gordon, age 45. She tells Horatio, "six months ago, the gun was used to shoot out a scoreboard at Antioch High School." Horatio says that Jeff is currently an Antioch student. Calleigh continues, "So I called the principal and found out that Ben Gordon, age 17, was responsible for shooting out the scoreboard. However, they believe another kid was with him, but because of the privacy law, they can't say anything."

Back on the B train, Miss Thing, whose name is Alison, is called in for questioning. She has a weekend bag with her cause she's going to be taking off for St. Thomas later in the afternoon for a photo shoot. Speedle regards this as a strike against her: her boyfriend died and she can still pull herself together to go to work the next day? He also asked if she moved the body. She says she did in the middle of the night.

Elsewhere, Horatio calls the Gordons into CSI central for questioning, and we find out that the elder Gordon is an overly permissive father. Ben is staring at bodies and Horatio approaches him. He asks Ben if he likes guns. Ben replies that they're cool, and asks him if he's ever killed anyone. Horatio ignores this question and asks if Ben and Jeff shot up the scoreboard together. Ben says he was acting alone. Does Ben know anything about the bullet-riddled tree in the yard? No, he does not. He wouldn't shoot a tree; he'd shoot the guy who killed Jeff. Horatio asks how he knows Jeff is dead. Ben says that if Jeff wasn't, he would have called by now.

Meanwhile, Speedle learns that Chuck—the dead guy—was two days away from marrying a woman who was not Miss Thing, and who didn't even know that Miss Thing existed.

On the plot A tip, Delko has analyzed the dirt in the sneakers retrieved from Jeff's locker, and figured out it came from a cemetery near Jeff's school. They head out there and find a decomposing body of another teenager—Mark Hubbard, born in 1986. Calleigh uses blood spatter and footprints to reconstruct what happened, and says there were three people present: the shooter, the victim, and someone else. They analyze the DNA found on cigarette butts at the scene and compare it to DNA collected from Jeff and Ben's discarded cigarette butts. We find that Ben was at the scene, and that a baseball bat bag was used to carry guns to the mausoleum.

Speedle has finished analyzing the pillow taken from Chuck's bed, and concluded that there was a facial imprint. He drags Miss Thing in for more questioning, and she says that yes, his face was in the pillow, but no, not cause she smothered him—because she did him from behind with a strap on at around 2 am.

Enter Ben and Nick for questioning. Nick is in denial about his son being a potential murderer. Ben chooses to remain silent about the mausoleum incident. Horatio notes that the bag says 420 Boyz, matching a T shirt found at Jeff's house, and asks about their interest in marijuana. Ben says that 4/20 is not only marijuana day, it's Hitler's birthday. Horatio concludes, "So we have Waco, the Federal building, Columbine and now Antioch. So you guys were planning an action, weren't you?" Ben explains that he and Mark decided not to participate; Jeff shot Mark, and threatened Ben to ensure his silence.

Cut to scores of black and whites headed to the high school, sirens blazing, to intercept Jeff before he shoots up the school at 4:20. Horatio runs into the school grounds as gunfire can be heard, and Jeff appears in a black trench coat . Horatio confronts him, tells him that his father took the gun rap for him and is doing two more years inside so his son won't be in trouble, and would he like to put a stop to this now, please? Jeff puts his gun to his head and Horatio tackles and disarms him.

Of course, since it's 53 minutes into the episode, it's time to wrap up the B plot: Speedle learns that Chuck was three times over the legal limit for alcohol, and finds one of Rena's fingernail charm imprints on the pillow as well. He calls her in again, and she admits to smothering him.

Then of course, we are treated to a touching scene in which Pete and Jeff discuss their shortcomings as father and son, and Jeff is led off.

Spring Break

It's spring break in Miami, and hordes of young people gather to do what white people do when given a week off from school: drink, black out, and drink more.

Anyway two guys wake up on a beach and try to roust their bikini clad companion to do the same, but her neck is at an odd angle, and her eyes are wide open in shock.

They get the hell out of there, and presumably call Miami's finest, cause the next scene is of Alexx and Horatio. They determine that she is a tourist, and her neck is broken.

After the credits roll, we see Calleigh at a party. She turns around and shows an idiot party goer her police badge and he backs off. She continues on her way and reaches the scene of the crime—a dirty, filthy pool with a young man at the bottom of it, and hundreds of spring breakers gawking. The detective says ""The motel manager called it in. He says there were a hundred kids out here last night, and no one saw anything." Delko adds, "It hasn't been down there long. It usually takes a while for the body to float. Body gasses have to have time to build up." They bring the body up and conclude that he may have been beaten, he was drunk when he died, and he didn't drown.

At the morgue, Alexx examines the body of Victim 1 and points out to Horatio: "At least six sets, avulsed. Most dramatic type. Bites like this don't just happen." Alexx swabs them for saliva, and as she continues the investigating the body, learns that the girl was raped post-mortem. And at the scene of the crime, a Michigan state ID has been found for a Rachel Moon. Although it's a fake ID, they are able to use it to trace her real identity, and learn that the girl's name is Tiffany Heitzenrader, 19, honor student, and varsity soccer player. Her older sister will be coming down to claim the body.

Horatio, meanwhile, has collected semen samples from the late Ms. Heitzenrader, and learns it belongs to Carson Mackie, aged 28, owner of a video company. Carson was convicted of statutory rape in 1993; he was 19, and his partner was 17.

Anyway as Carson is imploring the partygoers to flash him, Horatio appears in the frame and beckons him. Carson explains that he owns the company Babes on Break. The cops are not impressed. They ask him if he knows the victim and he says that girls like that are a dime a dozen. Horatio breaks it to him that they found his semen in her and she was dead when he did the deed; he protests that he thought she was just passed out. Which still makes it rape because a woman incapacitated—by alcohol, by a diabetic coma, by an anvil falling on her head—is rendered unable to give consent.

Back at the B-plot, we learn that the dead guy in the pool is 19-year-old Trey Hansom from Indianapolis. Cause of death: cerebral aneurism. We learn that some of the contusions and scratches on his body are recent, some not. So perhaps he was getting into barroom brawls on a regular basis? There is one bruise, however, in the middle of his forehead that looks fresh.

Calleigh and Delko pay a visit to the room that Trey was staying in. The room is neat—too neat for a hotel room hosting three or more teenagers on spring break. Also the boys are merrily pummeling each other, which explains the bruises. One of the young men suggests that Trey is off hooking up with some blonde from IU. Calleigh asks for the clothes they were wearing the night before because Trey is dead. They sort of gape at her and don't offer the clothes, or a response. Delko mentions that Trey's THC levels were off the hook, and kicks them out so he and Calleigh can search the room for pot, which they find.

In the tank, Horatio gets Carson to give him dental impressions and then greets the sister of the deceased. The dental impressions don't match the bite marks in the corpse, so they are only able to charge Carson with necrophilia. Speedle beckons Horatio to check out what he's found: an assortment of women found with broken necks while partying on spring break. They conclude they may have a serial killer on their hands.

Shortly thereafter, they get a call that there is a new victim—but this one is alive. They go to interview the woman, who was at a party on the beach sponsored by a tequila company, and she passed out. She was awakened when a man bit her really hard, so she kicked him in the head and screamed and he ran off. The swelling, however, has made it impossible for them to take an accurate impression of the bite marks.

Cut to the morons from Trey's hotel room in the tank, and Calleigh saying: "Here's what we know. Y'all were smoking out of the bong, and your friend Trey got very stoned. He vomited, and then he died." Delko asks "So the question is, guys, did somebody force him to smoke?" They tell Calleigh and Delko that they were in some sort of bong rip contest, and then Trey didn't feel well so they took him swimming so he could clear his head.

In another part of the lab, Horatio is examining the footage taken from Carson's camera. One of the ladies on film is Tiffany, who at first declines to show him anything, and then decides to in exchange for a tee shirt. The entire time she's on camera, she doesn't look at it, instead looking away.

As far as the Case of the Frat Boy is concerned, Calleigh and Delko look at the body again and notice that there are scratches on top of Trey's feet, and note that his shorts were on backwards. They surmise that his friends dressed him, but were too dumb toput his pants on the right way, and dragged him to the pool to dispose of the body without being noticed. They soon realize that they are being charged with neglectful homicide, and begin to appear appropriately grief-smitten.

Horatio is still looking at the Tiffany tape and notices that the photog had touched his lens with his thumb. Horatio prints the camera. He runs the prints and sees that the person to whom the prints belong had parking tickets given at the same time, and at the same beach, that the other girls were murdered.

The man who received these parking tickets is a Mr. Kip Miller, and Horatio gets him to give a dental impression. He then pays a visit to Amy and explains that the swelling has gone down so now her bite marks are useful, and could he please examine them? She consents but the impressions still don't match. Horatio gets Kip to remove temporary crowns on his cuspid and bicuspid, and viola! They match.

They cannot book him for murder, but they can book him for sexual assault. And that's something.

Tinder Box

Delko and Speedle are enjoying a night off in a club when the DJ's pyrotechnics start a fire. (Think Great White but with atrocious techno.) One exit is blocked, and there is only one fire extinguisher. Horatio arrives with the fire department and the building collapses, Delko and Speedle escaping just in time.

As the bodies are being examined, Horatio upbraids the fire chief for giving the club a permit even though two exits were chained shut. The fire chief protests that the exits were not blocked when he inspected the joint.

Delko seeks out DJ Scorpius, the person responsible for both the bad music and the pyrotechnics, and notes that DJ Scorp is soot-free. He says "Yeah, well, I saw the flames and I bounced, dog. I bounced", and says he uses the same pyrotechnics every weekend.

Horatio, meanwhile, is accusing the club owner of negligence since there were no sprinklers and the exits were chained, and wondered if the club owner set the fire to get out of a lease. Quentin—the owner—vehemently denies that he is responsible for wrong doing. He even shows Horatio the safe, which used to house $15,000 in cash and is now empty.

A few moments later, Horatio is pulled off the scene to investigate a hooker named Jill Susan who died at the home of a widowed judge. The judge says, "She seemed a little disoriented. Agitated. She asked if she could grab a shower. A few minutes later, I heard a loud noise. I ran in. She'd fallen. I turned off the water, called you guys. Can you help me? You know how this looks?" Horatio replies, "I do. Let's see if Jill's body confirms your story." Alexx shows him the body and says "No semen, no defensive wounds. She does have what appears to be a fracture to the frontal skull." . Alexx then shows him the soot on Jill's gums and says "You get this from smoke inhalation." Alexx and Horatio deduce that Jill was at the club prior to joining the judge. Alexx explains, "Smoke inhalation's like a time-release bomb. You walk away thinking you're okay. Soon, you're not walking at all." They run the registration on Jill's BMW, which is parked outside in the driveway, and learn it's registered to club owner Quentin Haid.

Haid claims that Jill worked three nights a week as a cocktail waitress, and Detective Tripp notes that she claimed $4,000 a week in tips, as did the other cocktail waitresses. Horatio accuses him of running a prostitution ring out of the club. He says he is not. Horatio says: "Oh, yes, you were. You were running girls. And in fact, even after this girl survived the fire, you had her go and turn a trick. That's who you are." Quentin says he didn't force her; he just lent her the car. Horatio continues "The thing I find amazing about you is that you have not inquired about her memorial service, and yet you want to know where your car is. That's pretty salt-of-the-earth. You know what? You can go. Go."

Calleigh and Delko then arrive, print some of the employees, gather evidence, and return to the lab so we can watch scenes of them processing it set to bad music. Calleigh plays a cassette tape that Scorpius used to record his set, and they notice the woosh of an accelerant. They conclude that there was rum on the curtains.

We also learn that the fire proofing was not up to code at the last inspection, but that Quentin claimed he fixed it after the inspection. This turns out not to be true.

They go to the club again and confirm that the curtains were dosed with rum, and follow the pour trail to Johnny the bartender, who is the only person besides Quentin who had the safe combo. Johnny has been stabbed to death with a broken bottle, and died before the fire.

Horatio then finds out that there was a strongbox in Quentin's car, filled with cash, and accuses Quentin of lying about his cash being stolen from the club before booking him with pandering.

At the club, they realize that the killer probably cut himself while stabbing the bartender, and that the exit near Johnny's body was unblocked during the fire. Delko, in fact, used that exit to get out of the club, and there is blood on the shirt he wore that night.

They do background checks on the employees and note that one bouncer, Danny, applied to be a firefighter multiple times and was rejected. They also remember him actively helping rescue people. Could he have set the fire to stage a circumstance that would allow him to show his firefighting prowess? Could Johnny have seen him start the fire and then died because of it? They take a sample of Danny's blood to match Delko's shirt. Indeed, it matches.

So he did it so he could achieve his lifelong dream of being a fireman. Quentin, meanwhile, has been denied his insurance claim because of the shoddy fireproofing.

Freaks and Tweaks

Cops converge on a rundown old barn where the body of a 25 year old man has been found. Horatio et al enter and note the presence of yellow powder, which leads them to conclude they are in a meth lab. The late proprietor of the meth lab is bound and gagged in a chair, appearing as though he was beaten senseless in the moments leading up to his death.

They linger long enough to find a box of porn so the audience can get their rocks off even though the victim this week isn't young, female, and half naked. When they hear a clicking sound they run out the door and the place explodes shortly thereafter.

Calleigh arrives with detective Hagan at a convenience store where a man has been shot. The man's wallet has been found in a nearby trashcan, and he has been shot at close range. Alexx arrives at the scene and it turns out she knows the victim—his name is Dennis and he is/was a family friend.

In the burnt out barn, the arson guys tell Horatio that the explosion was caused by a combination of dynamite and gasoline. They also find a piece of the bomb that will allow them to figure out who the perp might be. The body, oddly enough, is in good enough condition to be autopsied, and Alexx finds a shard of maple in the victim's head. Horatio concludes that he was hit with a pool cue, since he knows that pool cues are made of maple, because he knows everything. Speedle surmises "So we got two tweakers, up for days, getting cranked. They start scratching at each other. Our victim gets subdued somehow, bound with duct tape, and beaten to death with a pool cue." They also learn that the owner of the barn is one Judith Lindeman, and she rented to the deceased, whose name was Darwin Capshaw. They look up Darrin in the database and learn that his partner is one Tommy Lee Harkins.

Tommy is brought into the tank for questioning and Horatio taunts him for being on meth. The guy has a red stain on his shirt and Horatio asks if it's blood. Tommy says that some guy named Chaz got in an argument with Darwin and it got physical, so Tommy ran away. Oh and there was a girl there, but he doesn't know what happened to her.

On the plot B side, Alexx is charged with telling the kids that their daddy is dead.

Over in the morgue, Chaz has found a piece of paper on the victim. After analyzing it, he determines that it reads Chaz 555-0189. They decide that it's a cell phone cause "meth heads don't use land lines. They decide to run a GPS trace on the number.

He is located at a party and Horatio and the SWAT team shut the party down and order everyone present to get down and put their hands where they can see em. Horatio identifies Chaz fairly quickly and Chaz says, "I know your brother, Officer Raymond Caine. Well...I knew your brother. Big meth-head. God, he loved his crank, didn't he? You probably know that, don't you? Considering you had to do the mop-up on him after he checked out?"

Calleigh has gotten a fingerprint off a dud round, and identifies the print as belonging to one Brad Kenner, 22, employee of Sunrise Harbor Security.

Brad is called in for questioning and denies knowing Dennis, much less having a gun, not to mention using the gun to shoot Dennis. CAlleigh says: "Brad, I don't think you understand the evidence that we have. Ridge analysis says you, and only you, loaded the gun, and I can tell you exactly where you keep it. You keep it in your basement, or you keep it in your place of employment at the loading docks, and the reason that I know this is because humidity caused the primer to malfunction. There aren't a lot of basements in Florida, so my bet is, it's at the loading dock." Brad folds and says the gun belongs to his friend Julie

Harmon. This is the name of Dennis' widow, by the way. He was having an affair with her and she gave him the gun with instructions to shoot her husband. Alexx, who has been listening to this exchange, is livid. She says: "Why would she lie to me? To my face! Why would she have me sit there and tell her kids their daddy passed, like she had no idea why? My friend! To my face!"

At the trailer where Horatio busted the party, the cadaver dogs have turned up nil. He finds a notebook wherein Chaz has rambled on and on about "tin man" playing both sides. He also finds the bomb making kit. Wandering outside, Horatio sees a dog house but since he's a crime-fighting genius, he has deduced that the dog house hides stairs to a secret basement that hides the abducted girl that Tommy spoke of.

Horatio, as it turns out, knows the young lady. And the young lady used to do drugs with Horatio's late brother. He gets her to tell him all about what happened—Chaz beat Darwin to death and then abducted her and put her in the doghouse/basement. Speedle somehow matches pen marks on the duct tape to Chaz (they explain it but it's sort of farfetched and tedious so I summed it up thusly) but because Susie (the girl from the basement/doghouse) has written a note that says "I told you I'd get you back. You bastard. I hope you fry in Hell" the DA no longer believes her testimony. We also learn that Horatio's brother was on the task force assigned to get the haps on Chaz since he's been on Miami PD's watch list for awhile.

On the Dennis tip, Alexx storms into ballistics and tells Calleigh: "Did you see this? Dennis had cyclopentalate in his blood stream. 150 micrograms per mil according to the tox report." This is why Dennis' eyes were so dilated. She continues, "And who has access to eye drops, and who is an eye doctor at Coral Gables Professional Building?" Why Julie, that's who.

Calleigh calls her in for questioning and asks her about the eye drops. She says she prescribed them for migraines for her husband; the dilated eyes is just a side effect. Calleigh points out that blurred vision would have made it impossible for Dennis to see someone approaching him with a gun. Julie says "You're saying I slipped my husband eye drops before he left the house?" Calleigh admits that she doesn't have enough evidence to book Julie. But she does to book Brad, who Julie has admitted to seeing on the side. He will be booked for murder one.

Horatio has decided that since they can't pin Dennis' murder on Chaz, they can get him for attempted murder if they can prove that he made the bomb that blew up the barn when Miami PD was in it. Chaz is unimpressed. He says "Tin Man [horatio's brother] was a dirty cop. Who do you think taught me how to make bathtub meth? Got himself killed before anyone found out the truth. Probably went out squealing like a little girl." Horatio has him thrown out.

He talks to Susie before packing her off to Indiana, where she will be on probation. He asks her if she did meth with his brother. She says she didn't—well. She did crank; Ray didn't. Looking back on it, she presumes this is because he was an undercover cop.

Horatio sends her off and thumbs through the notebook he took from the trailer where he pinched Chaz. One passage says: "Tin Man's whack. Ask all kinds of questions. Going to get himself killed someday if the crank doesn't do it first."

Body Count

A man is shanked at a prison and Horatio is called in to investigate. He quickly figures out, however, that the murder was committed just to act as a distraction for a prison break. This is a pretty sophisticated operation, and three prisoners shoot a guard and take off in a helicopter. They identify one of the missing prisoners as Hank Kerner, in prison for murder one.

Horatio is torn from the prison, however, when Detective Hagen informs him that the chopper was shot down. Two of the inhabitants appeared to survive the crash and then were shot in the temple. Hank Kerner (murder and carjacker) and Randall Kaye (convicted of manslaughter) however, have escaped.

It is quickly ascertained that several prisoners switched wristbands, aiding in confusion as to who can be accounted for and who can't, so Delko and Speedle begin searching the cells of those responsible.

Horatio, meanwhile, is now on the scene of a carjacking that bears Kerner's fingerprints. The driver, a young woman who is of course identified as a mother, was shot. Anyway, cameras in the intersection picked up the carjacking as it went down, and Kerner has been photographed in the act. As was his partner, Stewart Otis. The camera shows that Otis may have been left behind and Kerner took off alone.

Calleigh, as it turns out, is the CSI responsible for putting Kerner behind bars, assisted by her lawyer friend Janet. She pays Janet a visit to explain that a convicted murderer is on the loose and may be after her.

Delko, meanwhile, has turned up a couple items worth noting at the prison. He thinks that Otis used Randall's daughter's picture as porn because the picture looks like it was taken up and down repeatedly. Also, they found red, white, and grey thread and decide that Otis is making a uniform so he can blend in with personnel at Emma's school and abduct her.

They go to Emma's school but it's too late. Otis has presumably taken her.

Dawn—Emma's mother—arrives to pick up her daughter. Horatio and Elena, without flashing badges or anything, tell her that her daughter has been abducted, her husband has broken out of jail, and ask her why a bunch of suitcases are in her car—is she taking a trip this afternoon?

She immediately cops to being involved by saying "my daughter was growing up without a father". Horatio then tells her that her husband's prison cellmate has abducted her daughter, and she needs to help them find her.

We then learn that lawyer Janet has been shot in the temple by Kerner. Hagen says: "You shouldn't be anywhere near this. If Kerner's bold enough to go after the prosecutor on his tourist trial, he's bold enough to go after the CSI. You should take time off until this is over."

Elsewhere, scent dogs have led investigators to an alleyway where they find Emma's clothes, and a pile of her hair. Horatio deduces that Otis is trying to pass her off as a boy.

At the CSI headquarters, Hagen has told us that Hank took time off his murder spree for a little time out with a hooker named Treynice, and her pimp is in the tank right now. They have her pimp call her to make sure she indeed was with Hank and he does, saying "Yo, delicious. What's taking so long? Where's my money? I didn't ask you what the bald boy likes, I asked you, do you got the money? Well, count it twice. I'm bouncing." As Calleigh comes in and learns of this secondhand, she accuses Hagen of trying to run the investigation without her. The pimp observes that they may be suffering from organizational ambiguity.

Treynice, however, hasn't gotten the hint and when the SWAT team enters with their guns blazing, Hank is nowhere to be found. Treynice says that he left to cap some blonde bitch cop, and referring to Calleigh as "Britney" points to the words 31 written on the wall in what appears to be blood. 31 is the code for murder. I like Treynice even more than I like her pimp.

Randall's wife, meanwhile, spills the beans on the exact nature of the escape and her involvement in it: "Randall said a convict had approached him about escaping. He wouldn't tell me who he was or what he had done. I should have asked. I told Randall's brother what the plan was." Horatio cuts her off and says, "Bryce, right? Bryce the pilot." Dawn answers, "Yeah. He would have done anything for his big brother. I called an offshore account in the morning to wire the -- wait. I remember one of the men asked for an RV. Randall didn't want me to be tied up purchasing one, so he decided to pay them both cash. They agreed on $50,000 apiece, which Bryce brought over on the helicopter. I don't know which one asked for the RV." Horatio says, "Stewart asked for the RV."

Elena is dispatched to see if any single men in the area rented or purchased an SUV, and her research takes her to the doorstep of one Simon Bishop. He claims that Stewart Odette, a friend of his from a chat room, borrowed his

SUV. Horatio says, "Stewart Otis. He is a convicted child molester and child killer. Did you know that?" In case this fails to ring a bell, Horatio tells him that Stewart might be traveling with a little girl dressed as a little boy. Simon says, "He said her name used to be Emma. He didn't tell me her new name. I haven't seen them since." And then hastily adds that he is not a child molester. But then sort of retracts it when he says "Emotional intimacy doesn't come with a predetermined age range. I merely challenge the accepted view that children are non-sexual." They arrest him for possessing pictures of Emma that are sexual in nature.

Calleigh, meanwhile, is working at the lab when Hagen stops by to check on her. She is somewhat offended and says "Not only did I graduate from the same academy as you, but I'm a southern woman and all that implies, and I don't know why you have so little confidence in my ability to protect myself." Ok so yes, she is a police officer, and presumably is armed. So I can see why she'd take his protectiveness as suggesting she's not competent.

He is understanding about the fact that she takes umbrage at his protectiveness, and explains that he lost Ray Caine and wouldn't want to lose another colleague. So she allows him to hang out with her while she processes evidence.

Simon, meanwhile, has been intimidated into telling Horatio et al where his RV has gone, and leads them to an Orange Bowl parking lot. Horatio pokes around with a flashlight and then finds Emma alive, under some plants in the field near the parking lot.

At the lab, Hagen has dozed off and Calleigh is gone, off to check out something she turned up when processing the substance used to write "31". The substance turned out to be A1 brand gun lubricant. Calleigh has, as it turns out, headed to a gun store. She tells the clerk sweetly if he carries A1 gun lube and the clerk says no. "Really? Now that's funny, 'cause it's this old-school lubricant that my daddy used to use, and I distinctly remember y'all [being] the only store in Miami that carried it," she says. He says he doesn't carry it. Calleigh shows him a picture of Hank; he doesn't remember ever having seen Hank but is looking more and more on edge.

Calleigh, meanwhile, is looking in a security mirror—the curved kind—and sees Hank creeping up with a gun. She tells the clerk she's just going to poke around, all while discretely reaching for her gun. She ends up behind Hank with her gun to his temple, telling him to drop it. He does. Cut to cops swaming the place to process him. As he is being led off, he warns Calleigh "this isn't over, bitch." She sweetly tells him "where you're going, I think you'll be the bitch."

As for Otis: Emma is drinking juice in CSI central and Horatio comes to talk to her. She is somewhat shaken but in good spirits, considering what she's been through. It turns out that Otis is going back to her school for a classmate of hers. The classmate is going on a class trip to the aquarium, and Otis has even had time to make an aquarium worker outfit.

Horatio arrives at the aquarium in time to see Otis watching his prey. Otis sees Horatio and another cop blocking both exits. He does the sensible thing: he grabs a kid to act as hostage and makes a break for it, heading towards a balcony. Horatio threatens him. Otis threatens to throw the girl off the balcony, but Horatio shoots him. He is wounded but not dead, and after sending the little girl to run down the stairs to the other cops, Horatio cuffs Otis. Otis says, "I'll just take another one. I will get out. It's in my nature." To which Horatio replies "and I'll be waiting. It's in my nature."

… CSI Miami: Season One

INDEX

altar boy............58, 63
antidepressants 14, 94
autopsy......69, 93, 96, 123, 124
ballistics 12, 104, 169, 216
barbeque...............173
barbiturates...........72
black box................15
blood pattern........145
boat.. 9, 29, 31, 32, 35, 36, 37, 38, 39, 125, 126, 129, 163, 192
bomb 8, 20, 21, 22, 23, 24, 25, 26, 27, 28, 175, 208, 213, 215, 217
briefcase....10, 11, 172
carjacking.....136, 219
cemetery...............198
chloroform.............22
church....................53
coast guard.............31
cocaine....32, 175, 177, 181, 182
courtroom.....167, 170
crime-scene tape... 66
crocodiles..............60
dental impressions
.........................203
diamond....55, 59, 61, 144, 149, 150
DNA 13, 27, 35, 44, 48, 49, 51, 56, 57, 59, 62, 81, 82, 83, 85, 86, 115, 136, 155, 159, 168, 198
dynamite...............212

entrance wound 53, 133
ephinedrine.....85, 86
explosive..........20, 24
Fortune 500............ 8
gasoline.. 59, 125, 213
Girl Scouts...........147
golf.......................173
gunpowder.....58, 192
gunshot residue 35, 106, 109
gynecomastia........ 30
heroin...................177
hooker..136, 138, 162, 208, 221
hostage................225
insecticide........27, 89
insurance..8, 116, 119, 211
judge.....110, 170, 208
Little Havana... 33, 37
marijuana.....195, 199
marina 81, 82, 84, 125, 162
Marine Corps.......105
meth 212, 213, 214, 217
Miami Zoo............160
morgue ..9, 10, 22, 30, 37, 43, 56, 70, 81, 83, 95, 104, 113, 118, 134, 147, 150, 155, 160, 167, 171, 187, 189, 202, 214
parole 73, 74, 148, 196
Photoshop..............32
pimp.. 47, 51, 221, 222
plane 7, 8, 9, 10, 11, 12, 13, 16, 17

polygraph 177, 179, 181
prison break 219
prostitution . 133, 209
psychosis 97
pyrotechnics 207
radiation poisoning
.... 155, 156
rapist 142, 149
retirement home .. 143
robbery . 133, 136, 147, 187, 188, 191
rosary 31
rum 209
security camera .. 108, 186, 187

security tapes ... 36, 70
sexual assault . 42, 206
Social Services 92
sodomized ... 147, 149, 152
stripper 161, 164
SWAT 112, 177, 214, 222
syringe 155, 156
tequila 204
tread mark 121
whistleblower ... 14, 17
wrench 60, 61

www.ingramcontent.com/pod-product-compliance
Lightning Source LLC
Chambersburg PA
CBHW031952080426
42735CB00007B/364